RIVER TIME

RIVER TIME

The Frontier on the Lower Neuse

JANET LEMBKE

Lyons & Burford,
Publishers

Printed in the United States of America

Design by Mary McBride

10 9 8 7 6 5 4 3 2 1

Library of Congress Cataloging-in-Publication Data

Lembke, Janet.
    River time: the frontier of the Lower Neuse/Janet Lembke.
        p.   cm.
    ISBN 1-55821-035-0: $16.95
    1. Neuse River Valley (N.C.)—Social life and customs. 2. Lembke, Janet. I. Title.
F262.N48L46   1989   89-2291
975.6'19—dc19   CIP

For Adrian, the Chief,
who brought me to the river

CONTENTS

ACKNOWLEDGMENTS

Most of the people who helped with this story are mentioned by name as they go about their river-lives on its pages. Several others deserve equal credit:

Mabel, Burt's wife for fifty years

Dot, our neighbor, who has seen the painters, rescued planks and piers from churning waves, and conveyed much of the truth

Gene Huntsman, sportsman and marine scientist, who introduced me to the polecats and the hogbears

Mark Mathis, archaeologist, who knows his chamberpots and projectile points

Cal Yaggy, president of the Neuse River Foundation, who does his durndest to open eyes to a large—and largely unseen—river

To all of you, my thanks.

RIVER TIME

River Time

Y OU WON'T BE a real river rat till you throw your watch away," says Mo, looking at my manacled wrist.

We've been talking about time, how it's told on the river in ways ancestral to the clocks of human devising. Life here is not timeless or without change, but it moves like a rolling hoop to aboriginal rhythms. On the river Neuse in coastal North Carolina, days and nights tick for us the way they must have for the people here long before we arrived in our automobiles and blue jeans—the colonists who did have clocks, the Indians who didn't. River time depends upon the circlings of sun and moon and the sweep of the constellations. The seasons make their rounds, directing the migrations of fish and birds, orchestrating the birth, death, and resurrection of the green world. Now from the northeast, now from the southwest, the winds blow constantly; they, far more than the tides, affect the river's rise and fall. Weather plays daily improvisations on a grand theme: brilliant blue calm, overcast, frog-drowning rain, waterspout, hurricane, and back to calm. The river burbles contentedly along the bulkheads or ripples with the gleam of hammered brass or rolls white-capped to

1

crash on seawalls with slap-cracking explosions that hurl white shards of spray high into the air and push dark waves of leaf-burning, grass-killing, soil-robbing salt water over the land.

We read our instructions. Time to plant beans and squash because the moon waxes and the leaves on the sweet-gum trees are new-minted green. Time to fish because the wind blows steady out of the northeast, the bluefish are running, the spotted seatrout are in. Time to put heavy-gauge plastic on the trailer's windows because Orion is rising, the ducks begin to raft on the river, and loons wake us daily with their yodels as they fish our nets. Time to stay inside, heat on, and catch up with reading because the pier pilings wear petticoats of ice and the ice itself catches fire when the sun goes down in a blaze that stains the whole sky before it turns to soot.

Conventional terminology is supplanted by days named for immediately significant events—The Day of the Five-Pound Puppy Drum, the Day of Harvesting the First Home-grown, Non-Cardboard Tomato, The Day of the Rescued Doe. Larger periods of time also bear the names they've earned—The Moon of Deer in the Soy Fields, when dawn brings the dull thump of hunters' guns; the Moon of Wild Cherries, when nineteen species of birds, including the feisty mocker, coexist in close, harmonious proximity as they gorge on the small black drupes.

Forgetting workaday time can, of course, be perilous. The Day of the Flounder Jubilee turned out, a week later, to have been Thursday the 12th, when I was supposed to have been subject to the ministrations of a dental hygienist at nine AM. But my husband and I were too busy carting away and cleaning self-beached summer flounder to pay any attention to such mundane matters. Dentists will wait; flounder, under pain of spoilage, will not.

We have television, three networks and a PBS channel, with more for those who have satellite dishes. The easily accessible stations devote little time to coverage of national news, and the regional newscasts tend to feature murder trials and sports. We watch because of the weather forecasts. It's important to know if the wind will switch from southwest to northeast because a change in direction affects the fishing conditions in our front yards. And it's important for me to know, especially in spring and fall, if a cold front is coming through because off-beat species of migrating birds are often blown our way by the passage of such a front. We have radio; rock, country music, and ballyhoo for the best car deals ever overwhelm the three-minute news breaks. We have newspapers. Those of national stature, such as *The Washington Post* and *The New York Times*, arrive in the mailboxes a day or two after publication. Local papers are delivered promptly—when there's a carrier willing to brave our labyrinth of rural roads. One of the biggest sources of information is the traffic over Cherry Point Marine Air Station, visible catty-corner across the river; a rise in the numbers of certain types of aircraft coming into or leaving the base often signals an international crisis before it makes the news.

The quality of river life is enhanced because geography and circumstance spare us from a cannonade of news and non-news dealing with matters we cannot influence. To say this does not mean that river-dwellers are lackadaisical. Far from it. Folks here vote regularly, volunteer their services to the fire department, take courses in CPR, and fly the flag on the Fourth of July. We read, discuss, argue, and gossip. The grapevine is the most vital source of information, letting all of us know quickly about policies and legislation—national, state, local—that affect our daily lives. The fire department entertains notions of building a substation close to the Point. The volunteers hold a fish-fry fundraiser. The state's Division of Marine Fisheries will change the rule about marking gill nets, from using one float of any kind at either end, to attaching two yellow floats for greater visibility. We avoid confiscation of our nets by tying on the requisite double lemons

3

fore and aft. Washington debates taxation or the disposal of nuclear wastes. Off go the letters and telegrams to Congress.

We're fortunate, my husband and I, to be able to live almost solely on river time. We give partial credit for that to his years of service to the U. S. Navy; he's a retired chief petty officer—I call him Chief—who specialized in photography during his career. Some small credit goes to the work I do when not living on river time; I write and teach, translating Aeschylus and Euripides. But the river and Great Neck Point receive the most sweeping bows for enabling us to survive on a shoestring. Water gives us fish and crabs. Earth provides summer feasting and bounty for the winter—tomatoes in dozens of mason jars, Blue Lake green beans packaged and frozen pint after pint, butternut squash laid in plump, tan rows out in the shed, popcorn for winter nights. Neighbors who keep chickens trade eggs for our fish. Hunting friends bring deer hams big enough to feed fifteen people at Thanksgiving and still leave sufficient leftovers for two small meals. All of us at the Point long ago joined the barter economy. The Chief has traded his woodworking talents for haircuts, and his services as a photographer for the labor needed to sink our pier pilings into the riverbed. We beachcomb, too—scavenging, some might call it—to bring home everything from crabpot floats to solid boards washed up the creek after a particularly savage nor'easter has torn down docks and piers. Once the river gave us a set of wooden steps to replace those stolen by Hurricane Gloria.

Deer for Thanksgiving—every day on the river is Thanksgiving, a source of something to be grateful for. And every morning is Christmas morning, wrapped in sun or pearly haze, rain or rare snow, a young day waiting to be opened. The gifts heap high. We discover that stingray meat is delectable. I see the hundred-and-eighty-first bird for the grand list of species seen in our environs. Mo's granddaughter K.D. brings me a snake I haven't seen before; I can't identify it till, a day later, the book describing reptiles falls

4

open by accident to the section immediately preceding that on snakes: it's not a snake at all but a lizard, a legless Eastern glass lizard. Dorothy, who knows how overdosed on tomatoes I've become after canning or stewing seven five-gallon buckets full, gives me a recipe that revives my enthusiasm; I make half a dozen pints of spicy tomato relish. The Chief shows his latest photographs; the hungry splash of the brown pelican diving for its dinner, the trepidation of the newly-fledged pileated woodpecker leaning from its nest cavity in the half-dead loblolly. The beach presents Indian potsherds; the woods, a swarm of bees. Or the river sends us a creature not usually found in its waters:

Yesterday, two days after Christmas: seven degrees above zero, and the river was frozen fifty feet out from shore. Ring-billed gulls perched on the ice; scaup and buffleheads swam at its ragged edges. Today, near noon: the temperature has climbed to seventy, wide skirts of melting ice drop from the pilings, and the frozen water breaks, separates into small floes, and turns to slush. The Chief stands at a window to observe this easing of winter's fist and remarks offhandedly, "Funny-looking duck out there."

Wings upraised, it's moving rapidly away from shore but somehow fails to become airborne. I get the binoculars: not wings but long ears! It's a deer swimming full-speed ahead. It must have entered the water from the sandy beach just up-river. We watch it for fifteen minutes, half an hour heading all-out for the far, far shore before it turns and swims this way again. It reaches the soft edge of the ice and barges through, making not for easy-exit beach but a stretch of wooden sea-wall rising vertically four feet above the river. Ten yards out its hooves touch bottom, and it wants to leap, hindlegs planted on the riverbed, forelegs lashing upward to gain purchase on the higher ground of ice but plunging through again and again.

We're outside on the bulkhead now. Bonnie has joined

us. The animal is tired, cold, and scared. Driven to the desperate swim by duck-hunters' dogs? Who knows. The Chief fetches a length of rope. Bonnie puts on rubber boots and descends into the river. Tying the rope around the deer's belly, she tugs it gently toward the wooden wall and hands rope's end to the Chief. While she pushes, he pulls, and the animal is landed—a half-grown doe. She screams hideously once, then is silent, docile, as the Chief carries her to Bonnie's house, to the warm laundry room by the back door. The little doe is wrapped in a quilt and placed on the floor, where she lies without struggle. Bonnie's daughters come to look and stroke her nose. After twenty minutes she rises. The back door is opened. She bounds down the steps and into the back fields. Bonnie pulls off her boots and empties them of now-warm ice water.

Sometimes the surprises are terrifying: the Chief, cutting grass along our back property line, stirs up a monstrous timber rattler. Sometimes they strain our slender means: low water reveals that a section of our bulkhead is rotting out; what can we exchange for the costly, necessary repairs? Sometimes they're merely unpleasant: the first vine-red tomatoes show blossom-end rot. Or looking up at a kingbird's nest, I edge close to the base of the pine in which it's built and find, too late, that I'm standing on a hill of fire ants. My shins are peppered with the buckshot of sharp bites. Longer-lasting was the surprise brought by a summer-day traipse through the woods on the eroded property just upriver. That evening I began to itch. The next morning, at least a hundred and fifty oozing bumps polka-dotted my feet, shins, thighs, crotch, belly, and arms.

"Mo," I say, "there's another reason not to wear a watch. Chiggers love to snuggle underneath the band."

"You won't be a real river rat," he retorts, "till you learn to call those things red bugs the way we do."

6

*   *   *

The lower Neuse—the name rhymes with *Zeus*—the lower Neuse and Great Neck Point are not among North Carolina's famed attractions. The Point is not tourist- or condo-country offering haven to fast-food strips, bars, and other manmade accoutrements of beach life. It's tucked away twelve miles upstream in a near-wilderness, little changed from that seen by the colonists and, long before them, the Indians.

The Point extends into the lower Neuse in a slow, three-mile curve of bulkheads and untamed beaches. Downriver the Great Neck peninsula is bounded by Adams Creek, now a portion of the Atlantic Intracoastal Waterway; upriver by Clubfoot Creek, one of the countless streams that wander through black needlerush and giant cordgrass to drain the coastal wetlands. Adams Creek and Clubfoot—the names figure on pre-revolutionary maps. The nearest towns are Beaufort to the south on Bogue Sound, twenty-five miles by road, about eighteen by the Waterway, and Havelock-Cherry Point, five miles across the water but twenty-two by land.

Close to the water, pines, sweetgums, baldy cypress, live oaks festooned with Spanish moss, and wax myrtle flourish in the sandy soil: typical maritime forest but tall and straight, unlike the oceanside version that's stunted and blown into bonsai shapes by salt-bearing wind. Trumpet vines, honeysuckle and snakehead greenbriar, Virginia creeper and poison ivy wind around the tree trunks and tangle high in the branches. It's a job to keep wilderness at bay, to grow green lawns of centipede or Bermuda grass, varieties that can survive drenching by saline water. A little farther inland, the earth is rich, dark humus over clay. Bordering the fields cleared long ago, hardwoods like maples, hickories, and pin oaks thrive amid the ever-present pines and gums. In the fields, we cultivate our garden plots, protected from the salt-bearing winds by woods and hedgerows. Joe has devoted half an acre to the melons that he shares with everyone; Al's made

7

a forest of speckled butterbeans climbing green and heavy-laden around poles eight feet tall. Not all of us are so ambitious; our smaller vegetable patches, bright with zinnias and marigolds, yield just enough produce, including good old southern collards and okra, for our own use. It's reliably reported that another crop is cultivated up Courts Creek, the Point's small waterway, where the feds and state troopers aren't likely to find it.

Water, brackish marsh, fields, hedgerows, woods, and gardens offer shelter to an array of aquatic and terrestrial wildlife whose diversity is increased by the Point's location at a latitude, just south of 35°, where southern and northern species overlap. They—and we who live here—have been protected from onrushing urbanization by the marshes and the forested wilderness that embrace the Point's fields and woods; landward, much of the Point is closed off by miles of pine plantations owned by timber companies.

The human community here is comprised of permanent residents and people who live within a small radius and come down regularly for weekend river time. Unlike some waterfront communities we have elbow room and more. The places on the waterfront sprawl out eighty-five to eight hundred feet wide, with occasional second and third tiers directly, discretely inland. One small brown-painted house rises on stilts in the third tier, out of a one-time tobacco field; the stilts lift it high enough to afford the young occupants a view of the river over hedgerows and rooftops. Away from any sight of water, other houses sit in shadowed clearings amid pine straw and oak leaves.

On the riverfront, *house* is a word that can be appropriately applied to only a few dwellings: Bonnie and Al's brick ranch that can weather almost any gale; the two-story cedar house that Dorothy and Kent built with their own hands. Tom and Merle's place, just downriver from ours, had its 1950's genesis in a superannuated school bus. The decades since have seen the slow accretion of a bedroom, a room containing

8

a real commode, and an attached storage shed for gill nets, a boat motor, and all the other paraphernalia needed for heavy-duty fishing. Most recently, Merle has been able to stop taking what she calls "bird baths;" after twenty years without, the place now boasts hot water and a stall shower.

Other people live in cinderblock cottages, double-wides (some luxurious), and the tied-down house trailers that manufacturers call mobile homes. The Chief and I, with Sally our flop-eared black-and-rust Doberman, live in just such an immobile home, an elderly 12×60 three-bedroom model.

Sally Doberdog has lots of company. Everyone keeps dogs, more or less. Some are pen dogs, black Labrador retrievers or reasonable facsimiles thereof for duck hunting and beagles or larger, rangy hounds for work in deer season. Most are strictly yard dogs that spend little time in their own yards and much in everyone else's. There's always a bitch in season, and a traveling gang-bang. Puppies are always tumbling at the heels of droopy-dugged mothers. Some could be registered with the AKC—a shepherd, a chow—but others mix the common with the exotic, Heinz 57 crossed with rottweiler. I know of only four house dogs in the neighborhood; one is obedience-trained Sal, the others are toy poodles.

Several yards contain chicken coops, and Eva also pens geese. Mo has stabled horses in his barn, and Jake the Dog-Killer used to tie out close to a dozen goats on his lot of less than half an acre. Caged mallards quack in another neighbor's back yard, while still another farms pigs, all of them named Dinner, in a wooden enclosure thirty yards from his house. Al specializes in California rabbits, a white breed with sooty ears and noses; most of them are also named Dinner.

Inland or on the water, almost every yard sports a pickup truck and a boat. The pickups are often embellished with a gun-rack across the rear window of the cab and a dog-box in the truckbed—testimony to the local fondness for hunting. There's always a mess of hauling to be done—brush, storm debris, aluminum cans for the recycling stations. Bringing

9

home the new appliance in the truck saves the fifty-dollar delivery charge imposed by the stores in town. These trucks are not expressions of machismo but modern-day workhorses. The Chief and I manage without a truck (we borrow on occasion), but we do have a boat, a modest fourteen-foot fiberglas Minnow that's propelled by an electric motor. A few of the local boats are play toys: some the sleek and superpowered hulls that can kick up long white rooster-tails as they're driven through the water at sixty knots an hour; others canopied platforms on pontoons that cruise the river sedately on calm days. One grizzled owner has christened his pontoon boat *HUCK FINN;* the letters are writ so nostalgically large that the naked eye can read them as the boat chugs by five hundred yards out. Almost no one sails. Benign wind and water do bring out a Sunfish or two and a solitary wind-surfer. But there's nothing here, not a blow-boat nor a stink-pot, that can be legitimately called a yacht. The large ketches and yawls, genoas billowing, and the blinding white cruisers with flying bridges stick to the channel on the river's far side. Utility characterizes our boats. They're small vessels for fishing, shrimping, and scavenging—shallow-draft johnboats squared off bow and stern, Boston Whalers for stability on choppy seas, sturdy aluminum rowboats like the dented sixteen-footer that Tom keeps next door. Al's yard holds a would-be boat, a beat-up fiberglass shell that he picked up at auction for fifty bucks. One of these days he'll get around to fixing it. The river is patient when it comes to boat-repairs.

Nobody seems to know much about the lower Neuse except the people who live and make their livings here. Yet, it's not a small river. What we see from our front yards is the more southerly of the two great rivers—the other is the Pamlico—that pour into Pamlico Sound. Way upstream, the Neuse is not a river but a creek, narrow and stained coppery brown by the humic acid of decaying bark and leaves. Much farther downstream, past the towns of New Bern and Havelock-Cherry Point, the mature Neuse bends like a giant's elbow and turns northward to make its final twelve-mile rush to the Sound. Oldtimers call the bend the Rounding of the River, and it's the place at which fresh water becomes saline, mainly because of the nor'easters that funnel water and salt-loving fish from the Sound into the river's gaping mouth and down its gradually narrowing gullet. Under a hard wind from the north, the river can rise a foot in an hour.

The Chief and I are the Great Neck Pointers who live farthest upstream, 861 feet from Courts Creek and the beginning of the Rounding. From our front yard, the far shore of the Neuse is nearly five miles away. Of all the wide rivers in the United States, our river, at this point in its course, is the widest of them all. Sometimes fog or haze closes in, the far shore disappears, and the river rolls across the world without a perceptible horizon.

Great Neck Pointers are isolated, inhabiting a peninsula that might as well be an island, cut off by water on one side, by a sea of green pines on the other. Nor is it just water and wilderness that separate us from the rest of the world, but the intangible barrier of distance from the services and amenities of urban life. On winter days, youngsters board the school bus before dawn and come home at dusk; the stop-and-start ride to the Havelock schools takes well over an hour each way. The providers of necessities—doctors and dentists, police and firefighters, supermarkets, banks, fuel suppliers, and more—are all out there twenty-two miles and thirty long minutes beyond the water, marshes, and pine plantations.

The river makes two stringent demands. One, given special force by our isolation, is for neighborliness in all matters from the borrowing of eggs and tools to rescuing the injured and comforting the bereaved. People survive at the Point because someone has a saving skill; people have died here because town is too far away to send help in time. The other demand is to honor the river with heart and soul. It must be respected both for the bounty it yields and for its power to devastate and kill. These commandments aren't always obeyed. We can be downright navel-gazing and nasty. But most of the people who have settled here have packed skills and a taste for isolation along with their household goods. Ralph Waldo Emerson would have approved the flourishing of self-reliance at the Point and of the way in which it's daily honed. He made the pertinent comment in his essay "Self-Reliance": "Your goodness must have some edge to it—else it is none." Isolation makes a fine whetstone.

As for my watch, it's still attached to my left wrist, more as a precaution against losing it than as a device needed to regulate the course of my days. Occasionally it comes in handy. But I consult it infrequently, and I stay out of the woods in red-bug weather unless I'm well-greased with insect repellent.

Right now no watch is needed to tell me the time. It's time to stop writing in favor of fishing our seven crabpots. With a hot-season moon bulging toward the full, the blue crabs come scuttling inshore to molt and mate. Last evening at sundown, I baited the pots with gizzard shad and set them off the bulkhead. The sun's now close to meridian. If the river has been generous, those pots will hold several dozen beautiful and tasty swimmers. The jennies will go back into the river to lay their eggs and make more crabs for next summer's catch, but I should harvest at least half a bucket of claw-clacking, yellow-bellied jimmies. Yum, crabcakes for supper.

2
Taking the River Road

Mo, who advises me to cast away my watch, wears the ghost of a timepiece on his left wrist. A scar exactly replicating the links of a metal watchband encircles it. The real watch attached to the real band stopped on May 17, 1960. The laws of probability say that Mo himself should have stopped, too, when 7200 volts of electricity coursed through his body. But here he is, outside his barn, tinkering with the balky starter of a power lawn mower. Or, he appears to be tinkering because he's moving slowly and chatting with me about his garden—butternut squash almost ripe, shiitake mushrooms sprouting at last. The mower will be fixed in short order.

Mo talks with the stem of a pipe clenched in his teeth, and his white goatee, trimmed to a puff like a rabbit's cotton-tail, bobs as he speaks. Smoke rises aromatic from the pipe—Carter Hall tobacco, the used, plastic-lidded tins of which clutter every level surface inside the barn and out. They hold the nuts, bolts, and spare parts of Mo's small-engine-repair business. As we talk, Sally Doberman plays with Mo's self-appointed guardian, a black toy poodle named Tippy. Sal lies on the ground and somehow makes herself small enough not

13

to discourage the tiny dog's participation in canine games. Tippy's rhinestone collar sparkles as she leaps and feints at Sal.

The barn is located cattycorner from the mailboxes and yellow newspaper racks, and I usually head barnward after collecting the day's news and correspondence. The wooded clearing behind the barn attracts avian species I rarely see elsewhere at the Point: a wood thrush gathering nesting materials, a palm warbler in breeding dress. It's the only place in which I've ever seen a common nighthawk or a hairy woodpecker. But if Mo is there, as he often is, sharpening a chainsaw blade or coaxing a garden tractor back to life, I forgo the birds in favor of conversation. Mo, his wife Joyce, and their children have lived on the Point for twenty years. They came here as pioneers of a sort, the first wave of non-farming "foreigners" to settle on land that had been tilled for generations by one family.

He talks with an accent as flat and broad as a midwestern cornfield. No kudzu southern drawl has ever sneaked a tendril into his speech, though he and Joyce have lived in coastal Carolina for forty years. Military service brought them here. Mo joined the Marines in 1942, flew planes now legendary— Corsairs and B-25s—in the South Pacific, and was discharged at war's end as a second lieutenant. When Korea caught fire, he was called back into the Marines. In 1954, he was again discharged, this time as a major. Joyce and their two young daughters were living in Havelock, the town intimately adjoined to Cherry Point Marine Air Station, and there they decided to stay. They bought a house and opened a hardware store. The first glimpse of Great Neck Point—and the house and barn that would be theirs—came in 1954 when they visited friends with a second home on the river. They had no inkling then that they'd ever be householders bringing up a family in the back of beyond.

Nor were they sure they'd stay even after they acquired the house, barn, and twenty acres of mixed pine and decid-

14

uous woods thirteen years after that first glimpse. The buildings and land had belonged to Miss Carrie, grand dame of the Point's farming days. Some of the house's present furnishings were also hers. I sit at Joyce's kitchen table in one of Miss Carrie's mahogany chairs. Made with high, narrow backs like those of bishop's chairs, they look as if they were designed to insist on good posture, but the padded seats invite long lingering. Joyce is putting together the ingredients for vanilla ice cream that Mo will churn later. She's slim as a bride, and petite; her clear skin shows little weathering though she's reached her sixties.

Joyce says, "When we moved down here, there were plenty of week-enders but only five permanent families, including us." She's vehement on the subject of the impermanent population, the people who owned cottages or trailers but came and went as their fancies and weather dictated. "Week-enders—pilgrims to nowhere—I want nothing to do with them. They'd forget salt, they'd forget ice, they'd want to use our telephone. Down here we need neighbors who do *not* mooch. Week-enders, they came down here for fun and frolic, but when it rained, they'd just go home. We lived here for better or worse. The road was so bad it had a 'farm-to-market' designation on the map. After a rain, you'd fishtail at fifteen miles an hour on that mud."

Nothing in Joyce's first forty years had prepared her for life beyond urban conveniences. "I never baked bread till I got here and had to go thirteen miles to the nearest dinky grocery store. I never canned tomatoes before—two quarts for each week of the year. After the forty-eighth quart, you're tired, you resent week-enders, but somehow it feels good. It feels like you're contributing something."

For years Joyce worked at Mo's side as an equal partner in the hardware store and, when he had his accident, tended it with occasional help from elder daughter Bonnie during his recuperation. The accident happened this way: Mo earned extra income as an electrician, and on that seventeenth day of

May, he was up a pole wearing spikes to hook up drops for a housing project at Ft. Bragg. Somehow a transformer used him as the ground for 7200 volts. No ordinary flesh can take that killing dose. When Joyce received the call from Ft. Bragg's hospital, she thought she would be driving 170 miles to see, at best, a dying man. But Mo was not ordinary flesh. It took six months at Duke University Hospital and another year at home for him to prove it. On his release from the hospital in late 1960, the doctors had told him that he'd be sterile. A third daughter was born to Mo and Joyce in 1961. And as before, they worked together in the hardware store till the late summer of 1976, when Mo suffered a second trial by fire.

Mo tells about it. "I'd closed the store at six o'clock and come home. The fire chief called from Havelock. He just wanted to let me know a fire had started in the restaurant a couple of doors down from the store. The chief called back soon to say the fire was out of control. It had moved into the auto parts store between the restaurant and me. Hydraulic fluid, oil—you can imagine. I went to town. They'd brought in the crash-crew foam truck from the air base, but it malfunctioned. So there I am out on the street just watching my place burn down."

Fire consumed everything, not only inventory but the store's records, including accounts receivable. "The tax people gave me one hell of a bad time. They showed no mercy." Nor did the credit customers. Of some two hundred, only one man came forward and paid the money owed. Mo expects people to be decent and honest; such larcenous dodging blisters memory more than the fire itself. "There is no place to hide a sin Without your conscience looking in," Joyce quotes.

The blazing end of the store meant finding work elsewhere. Mo embarked on several independent sidelines. For several years he fished on contract to a seafood market. He set his gill nets in the river, stretching them out from the pilings that supported an offshore duckblind. Friends helped him extract the catch every two or three hours, and in the interludes

16

they settled on the benches in the duckblind and played cards. Mo says, "One morning I took a big catch, mainly Spanish mackerel, down to the market. Till I arrived, they'd got maybe ten pounds in. Were they glad to see old Mo! I could lie and tell you I'd brought 'em a thousand pounds, but it was exactly nine hundred and ninety-nine." He also started a backyard farm for fishing worms, the kind known as red wigglers. He raises them still, performing a service to the Point by taking our expired refrigerators and upright freezers, items that would otherwise be laboriously carted to the dump. He tilts them on their backs, removes the doors, and fills them with a moist mixture of sawdust and ground straw. The worms grow plump on chicken laying mash. Sometimes the beds contain leg-hold traps to catch worm-plundering 'possums. Joyce counts out the red wigglers, seventy-five at a time, and puts them in cups that are peddled at gas stations and bait stores.

In 1978, Mo hired on at the Naval Air Rework Facility at Cherry Point as a mechanic's helper repairing H-46 helicopters, capacious birds with rotors fore and aft, that were designed to carry troops and cargo. Several H-46s, painted red and blue and indiscriminately known as Pedro, fly the river day and night as Search-and-Rescue craft manned by the Marines. Mo soon made it out of the helpers' ranks to full-fledged helicopter mechanic. How did he learn to fix such complex machines? "They're just like lawn mowers—they've got these little blades that whirl around."

On April Fool's Day this year, after more than a decade of repairing those gargantuan sky mowers, more than a decade of standing daylong on legs so badly burned that he could only shuffle to the nearest chair when he returned from work, Mo retired. Now he's employed daylong by tasks of his own devising. He can take the weight off his legs whenever he has a mind to, and he can tend his all-organic garden in the cool mornings rather than the after-work heat. Above all, he sets himself to his garden's clock.

17

"Thought you might like these," he says, handing me freshly picked leaves of sweet basil and sage. Filled with dark soil, the aluminum boat he used for contract-fishing now holds his herb garden. His latest project is building a structure to shade his patch of elephant garlic. "It loves cool weather, like broccoli and lettuce. It might appreciate a little break from summer sun." Mo sees his plants as entities as alive as he is.

Joyce delivers another bit of aphoristic verse: "Who plants a seed beneath the sod And waits to see believes in God."

Mo says, "Growing up on a farm, I've always gardened. When I was adolescent, it was mostly work. But, planting a seed, you can't deny the hope that goes with it."

One road leads to the river, Adams Creek Road, named for its destination, the confluence of that stream with the Neuse. Adams Creek is the address provided beside our names in the telephone directory. The road is narrow blacktop, bordered on either side by deep drainage ditches, that winds twelve miles in from NC Highway 101 and peters out near its end into dirt and grassy lanes.

It begins at a Mom-and-Pop store in Harlowe, an unincorporated, zip-through cluster of highway-hugging ranch-boxes. Shortly thereafter it crosses a canal first dug pre-colonially by Indians but only completed in 1828 as a watery short-cut between the Neuse and Beaufort. At almost any season, someone will be fishing from the bridge. From the canal to the county dump four miles farther in, the road meanders between the mobile homes and small frame houses of a black community. Its main cash crop is cabbages. They grow fat as basketballs in the rich, black soil, and when they're harvested at the beginning of June, the culls are spread free for the taking in the farmers' yards. People up and down the road eat heaps of coleslaw; residents of the Point run a summerlong exchange of recipes for preparing old cabbages in new ways.

At the dump, the black community ends and the speed

limit rises from 45 to a deceptive 55. The road twists too sin-
uously to allow such speed for long. Nor is the dump a place
to hurry past. Seven bins, their dark green paint flaking to
reveal spreading patches of rust, sit in a semi-circle at the
edge of a half-moon clearing in the pines. Someone with a
scolding sense of tidiness has spray-painted exhortations on
the fronts of the bins: TRASH HERE, BE NEAT, and DON'T
ACT LIKE A NASTY HOUND & THROW IT ON THE
GROUND. People often refer to the dump as the Greater
Harlowe Shopping Mall. If you can't find an item elsewhere,
you'll find it here. In trade you leave behind treasures for
someone else—a sofa with springs gone sprong, battered
crabpots, the metal cable taken off telephone poles acquired
for sawing into lumber. Sometimes the dump looks like a yard
sale, with clothing carefully spread on the rims of the bins or
placed neatly on the ground. The shoppers abound.

Another patron of the Mall, a small wiry man of indeter-
minate middle age, may often be seen as he climbs out of a
bin, puts his trophies into the saddle-baskets on his red bike,
and pedals away. He makes his living at the dump rooting
through rags and rot to collect aluminum cans. We see him
patrolling the roadside, too. The trash along North Carolina's
major highways is picked up by road-camp convicts under the
gun of a guard. But the way to Great Neck Point is a second-
ary road and thus a free-enterprise zone. The small man on
the red bike is proprietor of a scrapyard twelve miles long. He
does a good job.

The dump is also a drop-off place for used-up or useless
animals. Kittens are left in cardboard boxes outside the bins.
The dogs are legion. A mangy mutt, scavenging for garbage
that hasn't quite made it into a container, will slink into the
underbrush as we approach. Or a puppy still plump with
mother's milk will bounce up wagging not just its tail but its
whole fat little body. Take me home, take me home! The Chief
and I do not succumb to such blandishments, but other people do. The same dog is rarely seen at the dump week to week

unless the animal is so patently sick or hurt that only someone with money for large vet bills would consider trying to save it. Few people here have that kind of bucks, but many are willing to take on another mutt.

For two miles past the dump, farms dominate the flat-as-a-pancake land. Tree-shaded Oak Grove Methodist Church stands midway like a hyphen of whiteness between fields that push the woods far back on either side. On these cultivated acres soybeans spread lush carpets summerlong and corn stalks line the road like dark green walls. Before the corn begins to toughen and dry for animal fodder, it's subject to raids. We spot familiar cars and trucks parked on the roadside. The vehicles are empty, for their occupants have ventured amid leaves and towering stalks to gather as many young ears as they can carry. For a brief period after the kernels have begun to form, the corn is tender and sweet, and sweeter surely for having been snitched. Bluebirds perch overhead on the electric wires running parallel to fields and road. In fall and winter, they are joined by kestrels keeping predatory watch over the stripped fields. Deer, and men with guns and hounds, haunt the fringes of the soy fields after harvest. This county allows deer to be stalked with dogs because the woods may be so thickety that a hunter can't spot prey though it stands beside the next tree.

Long Creek and its bridge mark the end of farming country. Again, at almost any season, fishermen will decorate the concrete railings of the bridge or hunker amid needlerushes on the creek bank. They're angling for the panfish they call robins—really pumpkinseeds. Off the road, just past the creek, a dead tree offers a lookout post for red-tailed hawks. A quarter-mile farther on the left, a living baldy cypress dwarfs surrounding pines and gives its branches to the great blue herons. Sixteen slipshod-looking nests of sticks can be counted from the road in winter. In spring, twice that many slender herons rest or strut along the cypress limbs.

Six miles to go, and the next three are lined with loblollies planted by the timber companies and ready for harvest. For two centuries, pines have given work to this peninsula. An empty logging truck pokes its elephantine way over the hardtop as it heads for a pick-up of newly cut timber. The loggers, no oldtime lumberjacks with axes and crosscut saws and mules to pull out the fallen trees but men wielding chainsaws and driving huge yellow machines, cut several acres at a time. They trim the trunks and lift them onto flatbeds with vertical standards to contain the logs. Then it's off to the mill so that the wood can be pulped and rolled into paper. The logging operations sometimes take place deep out of sight in the pine plantations, but ears can hear the crash of trees and the high, warning *meep-meep-meep* as heavy equipment backs up. Other times, once shaded stretches of the road are opened to the sun. Brush left on the naked ground is piled and burned. Crews may plant seedlings with green needles no bigger than a dog's whiskers. Or real estate signs may sprout instead of trees if it's decided that development will bring more cash than pulpwood does.

Three miles to the river: Adams Creek Road is left behind. We turn onto the onetime farm-to-market road at a corner newly cleared of pines. Logging has not taken these trees. Instead, the timber company has donated the land to the Harlowe Volunteer Fire Department so that a substation may be built. The main station lies on the highway ten miles away, and its red trucks don't swim. After heavy rains, flooding creeks can bar the road to any traffic. Till the substation is built, people from the black community to the Point are truly stranded on an island where the woods and houses may go up in flame for lack of access by pumper trucks and tankers.

For two of the last three miles, the road seems a canyon winding its way through steep palisades of pines, gums, maples, oaks, and an occasional odd specimen called Hercules' club, the trunk of which is studded with large, protruding polygons of bark. Deer browse on the grassy margins and bound into the trees as cars approach. Once in a rare while, as

21

if we've hit a jackpot, we see an immature bald eagle hunched atop a road-killed 'possum. After the two miles, turn left again where mistletoe clusters high in the branches of deciduous trees. Turn again at the T that tucks Mo's barn under its arm to the right and wears the row of mailboxes and paper racks on its left shoulder. Go slowly down the bumpy dirt road, look right, and take a grassy lane. There's the river, looking as broad as Chesapeake Bay. The gulls are wheeling and crying over water that gleams like copper-colored silk moiré under a westering sun.

Guests, pulling up in our yard after a long drive from places inland, gasp at the typically flaming sunset and exclaim, "Oh, it's pretty as a picture postcard!" Picture postcard, my foot. This sunset is the real thing.

But when people come this far, they still may not have arrived. For the river makes its own weather, meteorological and human. It quickly sorts out the people who say Yes from those who say No, stunned by the facts of near wilderness— lack of fire and police protection, the sudden storms, the bloodthirsty bugs and venomous snakes, the winding miles that must be travelled back to the Mom-and-Pop store for a loaf of bread. No one straddles the fence and says Maybe.

"Pseudo-people can't handle it here," says Jim in his quiet, even voice. He sits in our yard as the sun goes down, burning the water, while he waits for fish to swim into his three nets, including a large-mesh flounder net that's receiving its baptism. Around eleven PM he'll untie his brown, flat-bottomed boat from our pier and row out to gather nets and catch. He's talking about city-bred folks on a back-to-basics kick, the enthusiasts who acquire a plot of rural land, get the good feeling of dirt under their fingernails, and run afoul of country pests and country plumbing.

Jim is the one person at the Point who makes as much of his living as he can from the river. His thick hair is almost black; his heavy, dark mustache shows flashes of metallic red.

22

He's in his thirties, all bone and sinew, as lean and fit as an athlete. No wonder, for he runs a line of two dozen crabpots spring through fall, he's out there on the river dawn till after dark rowing to set gill nets for blues, Spanish mackerel, seatrout, croaker, and whatever else he can peddle door-to-door along the road or take to the Farmers' Market in Raleigh. The nets spill smoothly from stowage in a trash barrel at the stern of his boat; he rows because it's too expensive to repair the motor gummed to inanition by inferior fuel. Birds lead him to his prey, the gulls and terns screaming and converging over one spot on the river, the osprey—"sea hawks" he calls them—plunging into the pond. When the river does not suffice or the weather blows rude, he hires out to practice carpentry, the trade that sustained him well until he and his wife Valerie settled on the river. He's connected to the numerous and close-knit clan with roots here, for his sister is married to one of Miss Carrie's great-grandsons.

Jim and Valerie moved to the Point at a moment that would have routed a week-ender or a pseudo-person. On the rainstruck afternoon before Gloria howled ashore, they pulled the mobile home filled with their worldly goods onto the lot they'd purchased only long enough before the move to have erected a toolshed and dug a well. The well pump could be operated by hand, but to be on the safe side, they'd brought water jugs filled for use in an emergency. The lot sits off the road in a clearing around which the woods press close and shady. Not a squirrel's leap from the clearing, Courts Creek begins in a narrow trickle. Jim and Valerie unhitched the trailer and made themselves at home inside. Darkness came early, and the pelting rain, the winds pushing with a force that close-packed trees could not break. There'd been no chance to put tie-downs on the trailer. It rocked in the gale. At midnight they abandoned it to the mercies of the storm and waded to the sturdy shed. That mere suggestion of a creek had risen, sending a foot of floodwater into the yard. Jim says, "I knew right then that I'd build us a house on stilts."

23

The house is now habitable, though it lacks exterior siding, and a deck to be attached later floats in the yard like a two-story island. Other, smaller dwellings—the houses for five beagles, two of the dogs for rabbit hunting, three for deer—are completed and placed at spacious intervals on the clearing's periphery. All are painted bright with primary colors, but no two are alike; one roof is rounded, another peaked, another gently sloped.

Valerie helps to support the joint venture with work at the kind of enterprises offered in the area. From small-town Pennsylvania, she's on the edge of 30, a tall, soft-spoken blonde with the spare figure of a boy. She's recently been an egg-handler, a nose-holding kind of job, at the chicken farm owned by the proprietors of the Mom-and-Pop store at the corner of Highway 101. Hammer in hand, she's also worked directly with Jim. Last summer, in the sultriest of weather, they reroofed a cottage near the water. One who observed them shakes his white head and says with admiration, "She was up there in the sun all day, didn't quit, doing a man's work."

Laboring mightily, putting hands on wood and fish, they touch earth and water and seem to gain strength thereby. Jim was born on a forty-acre farm near Marietta on the banks of the Ohio River. "I grew up with that river, spent a lot of time with hook and line. Learned carpentry there, too, when houses, then roads came to the farms around us. Somewhere in there I soaked up the Protestant work ethic. It still guides me."

When he rows out and fishes his three nets, the one that's just been baptized rewards him with half a dozen bluefish and one summer flounder that weighs a downright hefty three pounds.

Among the foreigners who have said a loud Yes to storms and snakes and distances and settled in, Mo and Joyce are oldtimers, Jim and Valerie late-comers. The Chief falls between, nor did he come so far geographically to claim the Point as home.

"The first time I saw the river was in '65," he says. "Came down from Virginia Beach to visit my brother at the place he was using. And my first thought was, Here's where I'm going to retire. You know sailors. They've got salt water in their blood.

"Adams Creek Road was tar and gravel then, not bad, but after that you'd need a four-wheel drive for the washboard dirt. When it rained, you could get stuck in the mud for two days. When it was dry, you ate dust. But that's where I wanted to be, on the river end of that sorry excuse for a road.

"That took a while, but when this patch of land came up for sale in '79, I had the money and I grabbed it—three hundred feet of riverfront and the god-damnedest jungle you ever did see. To get from one end to the other, you couldn't walk straight across the ground, too many trees, vines, deadfalls, briars, snakes. You had to go hand over hand, tree to tree, right along the river. My brother and I cleared it, with a little help, in eight weeks flat, starting at the back end so we could bring in the trailer, get the well dug, and install a septic system. We chopped all day and burned the brush each night. Those were some bonfires! The bulkhead was built right after we cleared the land."

They cleared selectively, not denuding the lot but sparing the bigger pines and sweetgums to shade the whole yard. They saved many myrtles, the leaves of which I now pluck to flavor stews and soups. In the back yard they left the wild cherries where birds feast in the moon that the fruit is ripe. Seeds of salt-resistant Bermuda grass and runners of St. Augustine grass were planted, and azaleas, air-rooted from the Chief's brother's bushes, were set beneath pines on the trailer's southern and eastern sides. Now grown half as tall as a man, the azaleas blush dark pink at the end of May. In late March, the King Alfred daffodils open their yellow trumpets; the bulbs are descended from some dug decades ago from the

RIVER TIME

Chief's father's garden in Whiteville, North Carolina, population 5,500, hub of a farming community and the seat of Columbus County on the South Carolina border.

Coming to the river was a homecoming of sorts for the Chief, back in his native state after years of Naval bases, six-month cruises, and taking photographs around the world. Scenes of Mt. Fuji, Moroccan mud walls, and flower-bedecked Swiss chalets decorate his albums along with the mandatory shots of grey aircraft carriers and ramrod admirals glittering with gold braid.

I look at my husband and think that his lives on land and sea have come together at the Point. He's put red cedars and fruit trees, two peaches and a fig, along the back line. The deck in front of the trailer is landscaped with yaupon hollies that he dug in the woods. He puts in vegetables according to his father's dictates: plant top-crops on the waxing moon and root-crops when it wanes. Keeping the same eye on the moon's phases, he advises me when to set the pots for crabs and eels. And he fishes, oh he fishes, at any time of day or night, netting enough to see us through the winter and still have extras to trade for what we need.

At night, sipping a beer, he sits in the cedar swing that he built and suspended between two pines near the riverfront. He plays night-owl to my early bird. Falling asleep, I hear the swing chains creaking lightly. Watching stars and the winking lights of the air traffic over Cherry Point, he's listening to the splash of jumping fish and the sounds of the river holding its endless, insistent conversation with the land. His imagination is hauling in fish and planting seeds. And he's grinning.

Whatever reasons for cleaving to the river, a certain kind of person receives nourishment here and thrives. But among these people who shout Yes, a few resident nay-sayers walk or skulk. Bad apples? Not really, for the distempers that bruise their views of the river world and cause them to decay

26

do not infect the rest of us. We speculate about these unac-
cepting souls and, in two cases, stand guard.

Most of the nay-sayers who live on the river are innocent
and amiable. Beulah, a born Tarheel with snowy hair and skin
as elegantly pale as an antebellum southern lady's, typifies
them. In a gentle voice, she says, "It's such a chore, you
know, to spend a whole day cleaning the cottage every time
we come down here." She and her husband Ed live twenty
miles away in town but come often to the second home they
bought in 1970. She makes it clear that she'd rather be cleaning her air-conditioned house and remain close to material
comforts than coping with pollen, pine straw, and sand, endless sand. In spring the pollen drifts on the river like delicate
lace, piles up as yellow mud on the beaches, and floats across
the fields in clouds as dense as those of a forest fire. Beulah's
nose becomes clogged, her eyes swell nearly shut. But here
she comes, pollen season or not, walking the lanes with Ed,
presiding over covered-dish picnics for the neighborhood, and
cosseting their grown, river-friendly children. She appreciates
the river but durned if she'll move down here permanently
until Ed gets the house just right, a task at which he's labored
hard but unpersuasively for nearly twenty years. And for
those loyal years, half of their married life, she's sighed with
resignation and tagged along because Ed, born a Mississippi
River rat near Cairo, Illinois, has always adored messing
around with boats and fish. Love for another person out-
weighs every grain of sand or pollen, every bundle of brown
pine needles, every fish scale the Point can present: not an
inconsequential reason for spending decades in a place to
which heart and instinct do not wholly assent.

There are other women, mostly of a middle-aged genera-
tion trained since infancy to be agreeable, who say No to the
river but dwell beside it because they say a firm Yes to their
husbands' wishes. The husbands figure in the bargain, too,
accepting wifely recalcitrance with a shrug and, certainly, a
measure of frustration. I don't know of specific examples, but

the river is bound to have acted on occasion as a marriage-breaker. It has definitely put the kibosh on many a real estate deal for which both partners were not equally enthusiastic.

The Nay-Sayers who merit capital letters are those who hold a stake in the quality of river life yet break its prime commandments: Respect your neighbor even if you cannot bring yourself to love him, and Honor the river, honor the other givens of the environment, land, wind, and living creatures. The Point has two who flout these strictures. They are unconscious of their failures to be reverent. We wonder about them and discuss their depredations but have never come within a mile of understanding their behavior.

A chapter in one long-running serial unfolds in the long, slow, sultry light of a summer's evening. Everyone in our section of the Point is outdoors to putter in yard or garden or just plain laze away a belly-stuffing supper. Jake is stumbling over the tires he's tossed into the river as he wades through sun-dappled water to fish the fifty-yard net stretched out from his pier. A galvanized metal washtub floats beside him to hold the catch. And he hoots, "Wooo-eee-hee-hee!" A dozen of us stop what we're doing and run, dogs galloping with us, to see what Jake has pulled out of his net. Well, looky there, a sandbar shark, a little one but a shark all the same.

"Don't see many of them things up this way, now do you," Jake bellows. He's slightly deaf, and everything he says bursts forth in a bull's roar. He looks like a bull, too, a massive, barrel-chested man with proud, thick haunches and bulging upper arms.

Some of us touch the shark's sandpapery skin. All the dogs sniff at it. As mild-mannered Sally investigates this cause of post-prandial commotion, one of Jake's two white geese rushes at her rump and nips. Startled, Sal whirls. Both geese hiss fiercely and scramble over Jake's bulkhead—plop, plop—into the water. There, with crafty insouciance, they paddle back and forth.

Ten days later our telephone rings. The Chief answers. I

can hear the caller clear across the room. "I'm getting out my gun," Jake shouts. "Gonna shoot your damn dog chased my geese in the river. They been there two weeks now. You get 'em out or I shoot. I see that dog over here one time, I shoot for sure."

The threat is not bullish blithering. He rock-bottom means it, for he long ago vowed to solve what he calls the Point's "dog problem."

For his eighteen river years, so people tell us, Jake has claimed to fancy animals more than most folks do. Like everyone else, he keeps dogs, two little ones that den themselves beneath the porch—the curly white Mama-Dog that wags when people approach and a honey-colored cocker-cross that doesn't. Jake points to abundant evidence of his love for animals: the two plump geese, a flock of scrawny part-mallard ducks that fend for themselves, at least half a dozen goats, and four hundred, count 'em, white rabbits caged and stacked in an open shed beside Jake's dwelling. Lolly, Jake's live-in companion, tends the bunnies, faithfully feeding and watering them and keeping orderly breeding records. Her care, however, and the shed's airiness do not entirely compensate for the light but pervasive stench of heaped dung. Because a third of an acre does not suffice for such a motley gathering of fowl and livestock, the goats are often staked out in the weedy fields behind Jake's lot, a process that starves them, for goats are not grazers but browsers that prefer to nourish themselves on shrubs and trees. We cannot tether them elsewhere, but by unspoken arrangement, we take turns righting and refilling the goats' overturned water buckets. And, as if such neglect were not enough, Jake's claim of love for critters is most damningly belied by an act he reiterates to the Point's ongoing rage and grief.

Jake is a passionate canicide, with Sal merely the latest mote in his baby blues. In the past few years he has shot seven dogs, all but one of them middling to large in size. Bonnie and Al's nursing rottweiler was among them and, a year later, her surviving pup. The most recent victim of Jake's twelve-gauge was a short-haired collie, one of a rare breed, that belonged to the fourteen-year-old son of a lifelong yay-sayer.

The free-roaming dogs of Great Neck Point do commit nuisances and worse. Of course, they bark and bay, the beagles in particular accusing the world of murder every time they lift their noses to the sky and bugle. The dogs dig ankle-wrenching holes in yards and race pell-mell through gardens leaving swathes of destruction down rows of newly sprouted plants. They flock to and fight over the bitches in season. And the packs pester Al's few rabbits, tearing out cage-bottoms and making bloody feasts. But, because we all own dogs, and all of them are culpable when it comes to raising ear-splitting rackets, we tolerate the noise. Conversation, albeit heated, can resolve other difficulties, as can fences that enclose gardens and electrified wire stretched around a rabbitry.

What Jake objects to is the harm that dogs supposedly inflict upon his beasts and birds. His suspicions are so quick to swell that he reaches for his shotgun even before a dog begins to trespass on his tiny farm. Nor does he shoot to kill. It is enough to fell the dog that might—or might not—be intent on injury to rabbit, duck, or goat. Al had to finish the job on his rottweiler. The fourteen-year-old found his collie dying two days after the event in one of the weedy goat fields. Human flesh is also in danger, for Jake's shots have whizzed inches past the kneecaps of people out walking with their dogs. The gravest injury, however, is that to human feelings.

The Chief and I will not permit ourselves such grief. Though Sally is a spayed homebody not given to running with the packs, the Chief stretches a wire taut between two trees in the front yard. Unless one of us is outside with her, Sal spends the daylight hours not unhappily chained to this run. We did not extract the geese from the river; in their own good time they clambered ashore and resumed their hissing, honking strut through Jake's yard. Still, the phone rings; Jake calls weekly to renew his threat.

But of the two Nay-Sayers, Jake is by far the easier to deal with. The other deserves neither name nor pseudonym. The man wields inanition like a hurricane. In the eight years that he has owned the acres of shore—clearing, woods, sandy beach—that spread upriver from our mutual boundary to Courts Creek, he has done nothing to conserve it. The trees at river's edge are so toppled, the shoreline so devoured that the unknowing eye would automatically assign the devastation to water driven by a hard gale. Without bulwarks, the land has suffered the lash of wind-incited waves for eight circlings of the river clock, for three thousand erosive days. It shrinks back visibly. If another hundred feet are lost, the shore will huddle along the row of old trees now separating the Nay-Sayer's clearing from the field immediately inland. He does nothing, nor does he often see his loss—water where once there were acres of land, for he chooses only to own the lot, not to protect it. He does not live here but cloisters his sensibilities five hours and a state line distant. Perhaps twice a year, he visits for an hour, scowls, and drives away. Why? We don't even try to guess. By his egregious absence, though, he is present, a ghost hovering heavy and premature over a deathbed. If the river were utterly remorseless in its demands for soil, none of us would dwell here. In the long run, of course, the river will win out, taking soil as it must, but we can fight holding actions with bulkheads, sand-trapping jetties, and rock revetments that will stay erosion for a decade or two.

We look next door and see something worse than lack of use—conscious abandonment. The man is the destroyer, not the river. Sorrowing, we turn away helpless and exercise what stewardship we can over our own small plots of river-blessed and river-threatened land.

*   *   *

How did I come to be mixed up with stewardship in the middle of nowhere? It's the Chief's fault. He was fishing with bright lures. "If you come down here," he said, "I promise you three birds—cranes, pileated woodpeckers, and pelicans."

He was courting, trying every enticement in his tackle box to induce me to leave the Virginia mountains for a visit to his river. We had met by mail two years before. A mutual friend, one of my former students, noticing that the Chief dabbled in story-writing, put us in touch, and we had conducted a steady mentor-and-pupil correspondence.

I was then giddy with freedom, back on my feet and relishing independence, making my own decisions, some of which sent me sprawling, after the end of a marriage that had lasted nearly a quarter of a century. My four children, two daughters and two sons, had fledged and flown: no more orthodontists nor unexpected trips to schools to deliver forgotten lunches, no jeans to launder and mend, no starving armies to be fed three times a day, day in and day out. I was responsible for no one but myself, and I quite liked it that way. My livelihood came through writing and translating Classical languages—Latin poems and Greek plays by Aeschylus and Euripides. Such work brings in enough for beans and pasta but not the rent, utilities, and taxes. So I also taught a hodgepodge of courses: community college classes in writing short prose and evening workshops for adults seeking non-credit entertainment with creative writing, autobiography, and marketing poetry and prose. In a medium-security state prison, I tangled with the bad guys, some of whom were good with words if nothing else, and taught them remedial composition as well as creative writing. And I conducted a seminar in literary translation for the prisoners' antitheses, a small group of young women who were graduate and undergraduate students at Princeton University. Such work—pleasure, really—was primarily self-scheduled and could thus be

32

put on hold if I took a notion to go to my rock on the Bull Pasture River for an afternoon of catching crayfish and watching birds. The Chief was right to use birds as bait. He didn't know, though, about my predisposition toward rivers.

In my half-century of years, I've lived variously on river time. During World War II, while my father was in England with the Army, my family summered at my uncle's log cabin on the banks of the Bull Pasture River. There, my grandmother, wearing a mountain woman's sunbonnet, sat in a rocker on the porch, her hands eternally busy mending rugs or stitching lace on pillow covers. My mother fetched spring water in buckets suspended from a yoke across her shoulders, and she pulled a wagon up the dirt lane and across the bridge to get groceries at a cracker-barrel general store. She always carried a stout walking stick, a snake-stick, in case she met a copperhead or diamondback en route. It seemed that my younger brother and I waited interminably, the river in constant sight, for her to finish her chores, make a picnic, and act as lifeguard while we splashed and slid down rocks slick with brown algae.

The Bull Pasture runs clear and white and often wild as it spills down its limestone gorge on a Virginia mountainside. It's located in the Western Range of the Appalachians near the West Virginia border, country that looks as if it had been crumpled into peaks and valleys by the squeeze of a gigantic fist. People say that the river got its name when Shenandoah Valley farmers herded their cattle to summer pasture in the mountains. The calves tired at the first river they had to ford, and it was subsequently called the Calf Pasture; at the crossing of the second river, the cows tired. The bulls, slogging on to the border, gave the third and final river its name.

My far-away father, like an Adam, had already named many living things for me—a great roster of birds and plants and farm animals. On the Bull Pasture I learned to see kingfishers, bass and rainbow trout, helgrammites to use for bait, and snakes to steer clear of. I tasted watercress, cold from

33

spring water and peppery. I turned over rocks in the shallows to catch crayfish and slid down a waterfall into the swimming hole. Lightning bugs filled jars on hot summer evenings. We'd set fishing poles for checking out next morning. At the age of ten, I came to relish thunder behind distant mountains, the ripple of sunlight on flowing water, and the constant sus- urrations of the river. I learned something of fear as well. Once a four-foot wall of water rolled down from the moun- tains, storm-spawned, and caught me unaware as I basked on a rock mid-river; it took an hour to fight through that roiling water and reach the shore ten yards away. Growing up, dreaming of a cabin on a river for my very own, I did not envision flat, North Carolina sand, a trailer, and a saline river five miles wide.

After two and a half years of sending manuscripts penned on yellow legal pads and writing decorous letters to accompany the stories and poems, the Chief abandoned the mail and picked up the telephone. Fortnightly letters became daily calls. And after several months of supporting long-dis- tance services, he arrived, with minimal warning, on my doorstep. The time was 5:45 AM. He had driven uphill all night, leaving the coastal lowlands, rolling into the Carolina and Virginia piedmonts, and ascending the Blue Ridge at Afton Mountain for the final, precipitous descent into the Shenandoah Valley. It was early fall, and the mountains had caught fire, maples glowing orange, oaks burning like scarlet embers. We explored autumn for two days—mountains, the Valley's fields, my rock in the Bull Pasture, and we both be- came sixteen again. I'd had no idea that two well-weathered people could fall so dizzily in love.

Of course I travelled south to see the Chief. At that heart- racing time, the wide, salty Neuse was merely a peripheral plus in the personal equation. Fifteen minutes after I'd arrived on a bright blue October afternoon, the Chief grabbed my hand, led me into the woods, and presented me with my first birds. They were not one of the species promised. From the lower limbs of a sweetgum, at the ends of ropes fastened around their legs, dangled two ducks, mallard hybrids, slowly spinning, the blood from their headless necks dripping quietly onto the leaves below. "Dinner," said the Chief. We ate them with gusto two days later.

Gusto had its reasons. The ducks had been part of Jake's catch-as-catch-can flock, fed only on what it could glean. And when these two had wandered into the yard of an essentially non-combative neighbor whose large but equally non-combative dog had been shot by Jake on its own territory, the neighbor found revenge. The beggar ducks, panhandling for tidbits, waddled over to the neighbor and touched his hands—hands that closed silently, firmly around their scrawny necks. Little is wasted at Great Neck Point, not empty paint cans, not the smallest scraps of lumber, certainly not food. The Chief, assuming a woman my age could cook anything including semi-wild ducks, had accepted them happily minutes before my arrival. Skinny things, but fortified with onion and celery, covered with strips of bacon, and roasted, they were succulent, and all the more so with the sweet taste of having done right by the murdered dog.

Jake asked a few days later if we'd happened to see any of his ducks, he was missing a couple. The Chief shrugged, avoiding yes or no. "Damn dogs," Jake bellowed and left with threats that he'd have to get hisself a few more of those duck-killers, yes sir.

Two hours after the introduction to Jake's ducks, the first of the three promised birds flew downriver—three "cranes," as the Chief called them before he acquired against all expectations a proper bird vocabulary. Necks tucked in, long legs outstretched, smoky wings spread wide, they were great blue herons. The pileated woodpeckers appeared the next day, gliding from tree trunk to tree trunk as they tattered the air with their whooping cackles. Brown pelicans waited till the following spring, when a lone specimen, head still clad in juvenile brown, alighted on the sandbar at the creekmouth and hunkered down for a nap. And the river came into view more fully with visit after visit, with fishing and watching the ducks raft, with rescuing the young doe from winter ice and seeing the warblers come in with spring and skinny-dipping in the summer. That July, after we had given the parlous condition of being in love nearly a year to dissipate or turn into something more substantial than a pink cloud, the Chief and I marched downhill to the church around the corner from my Virginia house and were married.

I found myself married not only to a scratchy-voiced, scratchy-bearded retired chief petty officer but to the salt water running in his blood and flowing in his front yard. I am still—will always be—surprised. It's not quite Indian summer in our lives; the first frosts loom somewhere ahead. This is a halcyon season, the calm that comes after years of child-rearing, the calm before infirmity overtakes the one parent left to us, before we ourselves lose vigor. Separately, we've both sailed turbulent oceans and found firm earth again. Now we put ourselves on river time and flow with it, no longer embarked on inward quests but turning outward to explore the world outside the boundaries of blood and bone. Log cabin on a mountain stream, trailer on a coastal river—the heart and gut respond to each in precisely the same way. It's not every middle-aged woman whose small-girl dream comes true.

I stand at the fish-cleaning table these days, covered with scales and good fortune, and I tell my husband that he's turned me into a fishwife.

"No, hon," he says. "A mermaid."

Mermaid? That's as good a term as any to describe my function on the river. Though I labor over canning kettles and pick endless pounds of crabmeat and do my share of fishing, though I feel a strong sense of acceptance and belonging, I'm more decorative than useful, like the rhinestones studding the collar of Mo's toy poodle.

At first, before I knew people's names, before they knew

mine, they referred to me as the Bird Woman because I tres-
passed everywhere, Sally at heel, pursuing summer nests, fall
falcons, and winter sparrows. Now I chase conversation as
well as birds. Most Great Neck Pointers are not so idle.

Bonnie, Mo's sturdy, square-built eldest daughter, talks
about their industriousness as she stands barefoot at her stove
packing snap beans in freezer bags. I loll at the high counter
that separates the kitchen area from the rest of the great room
and sip lemonade. The river sends a white glare through the
windows that face the waterfront. A ceiling fan stirs wet, sluggish heat. Steam rises from the bean-blanching pot, and
rivulets—cascades—of sweat run down Bonnie's face and
drip from her chin. "Do the beans and get them over with,"
she says. "I'll be glad next winter, if winter ever comes."

As she bags the beans and melts, she delivers a list of
local capabilities in a voice as measured as her father's. Of
course she mentions Mo and his small-engine shop first off,
and her husband Al, a metalsmith by trade, who can fabricate
anything from steel scrap—framing for the backdoor deck, a
pierced ladle as big as a dinner plate for scooping scalded
tomatoes out of boiling water, and whatever part is needed
for his tiller or his fire truck. Jim, our waterman, is only one of
several men expertly skilled at carpentry, men who can also
lay pipe, install air-conditioning, and fix furnaces. Kent, who
built his own two-story cedar house—the only dwelling at the
Point that could possibly qualify for *House Beautiful*,—erects
bulkheads with help from Al and others and, as owner of one
of the Point's two tractors, does custom work.

The tractor is a classic, the Farmall 1946 Cultivision
Model-A, with the seat offset to the right so that the driver
has a straight-ahead view of a field and the rows of tender
plants. For years it sat rusting in the yard of one of Miss Carrie's grandsons. Kent has restored it to pristine vigor. New
red paint glistens, copies of the original decals are properly
affixed, the rebuilt engine sparks willingly to life. Kent offers
the opinion that its exhaust-driven pneumatic lift may well be

the only one still operational on a Model-A anywhere in the country. He treats the tractor like the workhorse it was meant to be, pushing fill behind new bulkheads, dragging great concrete blocks to build a jetty, grading our dirt lane to keep it crowned and free of axle-crunching potholes. His wife Dorothy drives it, too, standing as a rider stands in the stirrups. She takes off her hat, whirls it over her head like a rodeo star, and keeps on chugging.

Bonnie's list goes on. The Point boasts a master plumber and a master electrician, both employed elsewhere but willing to rush their expertise to the aid of a neighbor—a neighbor, mind you, not just any old body who calls—for a trifling ten bucks an hour. And the clan rooted here has its own array of well-practiced skills, from putting up sheetrock to auto repairs. Nor is it just the men who perform necessary services at home and bring back the bacon from work. Many of the women hold full-time jobs—store manager, loan officer, nurse's aide, jet aircraft mechanic. At home, they not only raise chickens but hunt deer. Dorothy, riding a garden tractor, helps maintain the yards of neighbors who come to the river only on a part-time basis. And in her house, with a two-year-old son sometimes tugging at her knees, Jim's sister runs a combination beauty salon and barbershop.

Bonnie herself possesses what may be the Point's most valuable training. She's the closest thing to a doctor that we have—a state-certified Emergency Medical Technician. It's she who cleans wounds, soothes the hurts inflicted by jellyfish, and checks blood pressures. Because the rescue squad is based an hour's drive away, and has been known to lose its way trying to find us, it's Bonnie who rides along barefoot to monitor and comfort someone being rushed by private vehicle to an emergency room. At the behest of a nurses' registry, she does sometimes put on shoes, along with a white uniform, and takes night duty tending usually terminal patients.

The beans are packaged, the counter is heaped with bulging bags. "Outstanding," Bonnie says, giving herself a well-earned pat on the back. She stores them in the freezer, grabs a paperback novel and a tall, icy lemonade, and heads for a good long soak in the tub.

Sophisticated knowledge of practical matters, well-honed skills, hands-on experience—these are not the only qualities I see that sustain the Point. Wit and ingenuity play a part. Mo once assured his household of a continuing supply of water during frequent power-outages. No electricity, no way to put well water into the storage tank, except that Mo rigged up a simple means of using muscle power when the manmade lightning failed: a bicycle pump. And the son of our next-door neighbors Tom and Merle contrived a boat hoist as his father's birthday present: the boom and winch come from conventional sources, but an office machine provided the half-horse motor that drives the winch. The hoist has been christened Leroy.

I believe that week-enders and pseudo-people really couldn't handle this. Nor do some of the folks who live halfway to town on Highway 101, folks in circumstances only minimally less rural than ours, seem to understand what keeps us here on the edge of the world. We face the river. They face the road, as one elderly lady, a lifelong resident in nearby parts, thinks folks are supposed to do. She asks with utter puzzlement, "Wha'chew doin' livin' out there with the polecats and the hawgbears?"

The coast has known the human presence for more than a thousand years. The Indians of many tribes camped on these shores and left behind their cookpots, arrowheads, and amulets and cast their emptied oyster shells into heaping middens. Some of the shells are nine-plus inches long; oysters nowadays are harvested long before they reach this size. The Indians fished here for the same species that we catch and hunted deer and bear. Just inland, where timber-company pines reach upward thick and tall, they cleared patches of woodland for villages and gardens where they raised crops

still familiar—corn, squash, beans, and tobacco. European ex-
plorers arrived late in the 1500s, and by the beginning of the
eighteenth century, the settlers came en masse. New Bern,
second oldest town in North Carolina, received its first colonists in 1710. By now, three hundred years after the advent of
Englishmen and settlers from the Palatinate, you'd think isolation would have ended. It hasn't.

A great to-do is made about the Carolina coast these
days. Typical—and quite action-worthy—matters for discus-
sion include dealing with a certainly rising sea level, reducing
pollution, and assuring the health and safety of shellfish beds.
The perception of Great Neck Pointers, however, is that the
talk and the seminars, the lobbying and the legislation focus
on coastal places such as the Outer Banks, the Sounds, and
the tidal estuaries that serve as the nurseries essential to marine life. Small-craft warnings are issued for those parts of the
coast but not for the rivers. It is as if our part of the lower
Neuse—this vast expanse of teeming, salty water—does not
exist. Or, it exists only as the locus for some kiddy sailing
camps, quaint towns for tourists, and jet-loud Cherry Point.
In quickly disappearing flashes of attention, the media notice
the Neuse and its northerly sister the Pamlico only if the
phosphate-mining operation on the Pamlico applies for a new
waste-water permit or a tank in the pulp mill upstream on the
Neuse explodes or commercial fishermen see disease or a de-
cline in the catch—or someone drowns. New Bern itself, at
the head of the lower Neuse, is not the bustling port of 1900,
second busiest in the state, but a quietly congenial backwater
town.

We feel ignored, though we're hardly complaining.
Escaping notice has its benefits. But is the impression that official eyes see everything but the river a misimpression?
"No," says a local fisherman and hunter who is also a scientist for the National Marine Fisheries Service. "That perception is good, solid, real, honest."

Who, then, chooses polecats, hogbears, and invisibility?

Working people mostly, some highly educated, some not, who come primarily from small towns and farms. Many have known poverty as intimately as they knew their mothers' arms. Great Neck Pointers are people with an affinity for earth and water. Cussedly self-reliant people with a sharp edge to their goodness; people who nominally fit the acronym WASP but to whom its pejorative sting cannot be applied. People zealous to keep the commandments of neighborliness and respect for the river. Bonnie probably zeroes in on the one absolute requirement for staying at road's end and setting mortal rhythms to the river's timeless clock: "To live in a place where you can expect to be alone, you're going to be your own company, and you've got—you have *got* to like yourself."

3

Living with the Polecats and the Hogbears

I
N THE MIDDLE of a warm Sunday morning, a float plane lands on the water five hundred yards downriver.

How can I who live on river time name the day? Because, apart from the plane's arrival, a calm prevails, a brief quietus in the noisy work and recreation that the lower Neuse affords. It is the time for attending, or not attending, church, and those who choose to avoid the sacred precincts make themselves scarce, sleeping late or watching a rental movie on the VCR. Al, obeying some internal call to diligence, may be found outside worshipping his garden with a hoe. Aside from the crabmen unobtrusively tending their pots, commerce rests; the trawlers are kept by law from pulling nets during Sunday's daylit hours. Come dusk, however, the low, steady drone of their straining engines will again be heard. The week-end sportsmen also rest. Most of the sails that have flecked the Saturday water far offshore are furled till afternoon, and the water-skiers—not local people who understand what buoys are—also wait to resume their inshore games amid the gill nets and the commercial crablines.

The float plane's appearance brings people out of their Sunday torpor. We congregate on the bulkheads to look and speculate. Everyone recognizes the aircraft: it's operated by the enforcement section of the state's Division of Marine Fisheries. We see it infrequently but know that its descent means bad news for someone. Today it's lingering, rocking gently on its pontoons. I run for my binoculars, but by the time I return to our bulkhead, the Chief's far-sighted eyes have ascertained the float plane's purpose. It's confiscating a net, a two-hundred yarder. We walk downriver, closer to the action, and meet Dorothy who knows the whole tale.

"Fisheries is taking the net," she says, "because it's not legally marked, no double yellow floats on either end. The guys who set it were using plastic milk jugs."

But it's Sunday, an odd time for Fisheries' enforcement branch, strict though it is, to be out here seizing a net. Nor did the plane patrol the area first. It simply descended out of the clear blue Sunday sky.

Dorothy collects the Point's news as a gill net collects fish. It swims into her ken because she pauses to chat with everyone she encounters on her Point-encompassing daily walk. She asks forthright questions, a practice she describes as "not nosy—you call it being neighborly." This morning, people were entirely glad to tell her about the net now being hauled, yard after yard, into the float plane's cabin.

"It's an act of satisfaction," she says. "Satisfaction, pure, simple, and oh so sweet." She grins.

It seems that a cottage, the one near the pilings where the double-crested cormorants perch, was bought by someone from Raleigh maybe a month ago. Last night, about midnight, he finally arrived with a couple of buddies and a boat, making a hullabaloo that just kept getting louder. About three in the morning this raucous crew had decided that the thing to do

43

was set a net. So, they'd driven to the boat ramp, launched the boat, climbed aboard, and sunk it.

Dorothy says, "The man next-door to the ramp tells me it took them a whole hour of shouting to bail the boat out with its tarp. They eventually got off, though, set the net, and came back loud as ever. Man next to the ramp asked them please, be quiet, he was trying to sleep. They didn't listen. So, he got his gun and fired a couple of shots in the air. They calmed down and left—but came back two hours later at dawn. They were going out to fish the net. But the boat motor wouldn't start because, dummies, they'd covered it with the wet tarp they'd bailed the boat with. You can just hear it— more racket, more damnation. The man by the ramp called Fisheries."

We agree that justice has been served in both its public and private capacities. Not only have these inlanders forfeited several hundred dollars' worth of gill net, but they've been given citations mandating a court appearance that will probably lead to payment of a not inconsequential fine. The kicker is that if they had committed their illegalities with a decorum that respected others' sleep, they would not have triggered the call to Fisheries. The float plane would have honored the Sabbath by remaining at its mooring. But, as is, the unwilling insomniac has gained personal satisfaction in a way entirely compatible with formal maintenance of law and order. The magnitude of his rage is measured by the fact that he contacted Fisheries on a day of rest.

The noisy celebrators ran into a polecat all right, the kind that sprays the air with bullets. But what is a hogbear? I ask around. Turns out that the double-barreled phrase is a near-cliché, a term with color but little substance; no one has paid it much mind. Attempts are made though, to define the second member of the term. They range from "something like a heffalump" to "bugbear, bugaboo"—from a bumbling and harmless creature of the mind to an equally imaginary incarnation of the terrors that lurk in the deep, dark woods as sea serpents lurk in the lightless oceans. Hogbear seems a word of connotation, denoting nothing.

The world of watches and schedules lies half an hour's drive away, not truly far in time or miles but distant as Erehwon in terms of its attitudes. We go to it; it does not often come to us. Fire departments, sheriff's men, rescue squads, the doctors and the lawyers ply their business elsewhere, venturing our way only in the gravest or most lucrative emergencies. The state's official road map fails to notice Harlowe, much less Great Neck Point. The latter name does appear on the Federal Defense Mapping Agency's 1975 topographic quadrangle and on the National Oceanic and Atmospheric Administration's 1986 nautical chart of the lower Neuse. On both of these maps, Great Neck Point designates a geographic location rather than a human community, and the Point's land looks virtually uninhabited, a waste transected by many creeks and marshes but few roads. The maps do not concur about the name of our creek; the chart opts for Courts, the quadrangle for Coaches. Local opinion holds that the chart shows the colonial name; it was transmogrified on southern tongues that shun the letter *r* but relish the reduplication of *s*: Courts to Co'ts to Co'tses to Coaches.

As the Point's most salient offshore features, the nautical chart shows a sunken wreck and a submerged obstruction. The wreck, a hodgepodge of ballast and wormy timbers, is situated in the Chief's and my underwater yard, just off the end of our pier. As for the obstruction, it's a thousand-gallon fuel tank that's only half submerged when the frequent southwesterlies cause the level of the river to fall; snapping turtles sun themselves atop the tank's corroded metal, and greenbacked herons strut there hunting for minnows. This year, in a typical Great Neck Point gesture of self-interest, Dorothy and Kent affixed a styrofoam float to the tank to mark its position during spells of high water. And they've put similar warnings on other underwater hull-rippers.

The Point, if it's noticed at all, is given only the most cursory nod. Out here, unincorporated, unsupervised, we are even beyond the pale of government at times. Despite the countless years that people have traversed its sandy shore, that log canoes, squareriggers, and steamships have passed by on the water road, the Point is still a frontier. Its enthusiasts handle problems with frontier pragmatism. Sometimes ignorance or ingrained myth supports impromptu action; sometimes necessity leads the way or, as with the man unwillingly waked, a flame of righteous rage.

The Chief and I join Tom and his longtime fishing friend Burt as they sit in Tom's yard looking at the twilit river. They've just set three nets, one deep for blues and Spanish mackerel, one for flounder off the Nay-Sayer's eroded land, the third by the spot-hole just upriver from the creek.

Burt shells a peanut and pops it into his mouth. "Hogbear? He's a bear like we got around here. Not grizzly, we ain't got none of them. But some in the forest behind my house weigh a good four hundred pound. I saw one on the train tracks spanned those rails. I wouldn't mess around with them."

He shells and pops another peanut and tells us then about a truly extraordinary creature, a hybrid, that he's damn' sure encountered in the woods. "You hear about the poplarleaf snake? That's when a black snake and a rattlesnake is mixin'."

Folk-belief flourishes here. Nothing shows this phenomenon more clearly than the refusal of at the Point to look a certain kind of gift horse in the mouth. Our gift horse is a deer. Al tells a story from his early days on the river. "Bonnie and I had just gone to bed, nice and peaceful. We were still finishing our house, and the bedroom walls had nothing but insula-

46

tion on 'em—that fibreglas stuff with a shiny silver backing. All of a sudden the room lit up, crazy lights bouncing up and down that silver, getting bigger and brighter—car headlights. Someone was speeding up and down the potholes of our lane. The car stopped in our yard, the door opened, and I heard a yell for help. Well, I pulled on my pants and found my slippers right quick. There was a neighbour standing there non-stop hollering. She opened the boot of her car. All I could see were eyes. O Lord, I thought, she's gone and killed somebody, now what? Nope, she'd hit a buck deer on her way home. Big woman, she wrestled that deer into the boot. What she wanted was me to help her dress it out."

Fresh meat—that's the point, not notifying the wildlife officer, which is the title bestowed on our game wardens. Nor is vehicle hitting deer on the last, well-wooded stretch of road strictly an event of years past. It happens several times each year, and people have been known to go out of their way to do it. If the deer is dead or unconscious, it's heaved immediately into trunk or truckbed or, with some risks, the back seat. Bonnie learned about the risks when she struck a half-grown fawn and manhandled its limp, bleeding body into her hatchback Mustang. "I was sure I'd killed it. But a mile down the road that bambi woke up. It struggled and it thrashed, long legs all over the place. It was like having a wrecking ball inside my car. Only one thing to do: stop car, get out, slam door, and walk that last mile home. Al finished the job I'd started."

It is a willful flouting of regulations not to report such out-of-season kills. Non-compliance is prompted, however, by more than an understandable yen for deer meat, by more than a policy of waste not, want not. A myth has arisen: people *know* that the warden will confiscate such kills, and they also know with unbudgeable firmness that the warden himself will feast merrily on what he has taken from those whose vehicles are bashed and bloody.

These beliefs are potent, if not justified. But learning the truth presents frustrating, time-consuming complications. I've checked with the state and local agencies to see what the regulations call for. The Wildlife Commission's headquarters in Raleigh advises calling the local Department of Transportation, and the woman answering my queries to the Commission says that DOT will bury the deer or give it away. Give it to whom? She doesn't know. I call the county's DOT office, and another woman says, "Yes, we'll fetch it and bury it *if* we're notified and *if* the deer is on a state-maintained road." DOT does not give carcasses away to anyone; the earth receives them all. I tell the woman at DOT that local people take their road-kills home to eat, and she responds, "Aw, I couldn't handle that." She does tell me that the Highway Patrol, rather than the lone citizen, is the greatest source of dead-deer reports, for owners of battered vehicles call the troopers so that auto damage may be officially assessed—the first step in collecting on insurance. As for notifying the district's wildlife officer, his phone number is not listed in our directory but must be obtained from headquarters. And when the local digits have been scribbled down and dialed, an answering machine may bid the caller leave a name and number to be contacted later. I leave a message; my call is not returned.

When I do reach the game warden a week later, he furnishes the long-sought facts. In or out of season a driver may obtain a permit to possess a struck-down deer. All that's needed is a call to the police, the sheriff's department, or the state troopers, for the Wildlife Commission gives permit-forms to all local law-enforcement agencies so that dead deer can be dealt with on the scene at any time of night or day. If the driver doesn't want the deer, statutes allow an edible carcass to be donated to an organization serving the needy. Inmates of prison road-camps are frequent recipients of such contributions. And how about the popular belief that wardens keep such deer for personal use? Our district officer rears back. "We're *very* strict about illegal possession. Officers are not willing to jeopardize their jobs for a piece of meat."

I take him at his word.

"I've been thinking about that hogbear," Tom says. "Like Burt told you, it's the bear we've got around here. It roots in the woods and grunts."

Now we're getting somewhere. Denotation begins to come clear. I see a bear, its piglike shoulders low, its rump ascending, as it shuffles through mast on the forest floor. But I'm not quite satisfied.

Just as we live with hogbears grunting through the woods, we live with their acquatic equivalents. The Point treats regulations covering marine affairs with the same cavalier practicality as those that deal with inland game. We police the water not just by summoning authority but by unauthorized enforcement of the rules.

Mid-morning on a recent weekday, someone in an unfamiliar white boat with a blue motor set gill nets, one off the eroded shore next door, the other just upriver of the creek. No one tended them the next day or the next, though regulations state that a gill net must be checked at least once every twenty-four hours that it remains in the water. Through Saturday's bustle and Sunday's somnolence there was no sign of white boat with blue motor. At new week's beginning, after supper, the Chief and I borrow Tom's boat for a look at the nearer net. The requisite pairs of yellow floats bob at either end, but the corkline is invisible, pulled beneath the surface by the weight of death. We take the two hundred yards ashore and spend two reeking hours extracting rotten flounder, spot, croaker, blues, Spanish mackerel, menhaden, and one gigantic cow-nosed ray. Even Sally, who delights in raw fish, refuses after one sniff to touch this putrefaction. The only life entangled in the filaments is blue crab—ten fat jimmies coming inshore to look for hidey-holes in which to molt. I know they're close to molting because when I clean them I find that each hard shell conceals a new integument as light and tough as plastic film. Their meat sits packaged neatly in the freezer now. The next evening, Tom and Al retrieve the second net, which proves to be two hundred-yarders set back to back. They also sag with death. The styrofoam floats on all the nets are carved with the name and address of a purported owner in town, but the phone book lists no such name, nor can we learn who might be at the address given. On an errand-run to town, Al drives past the house; it sits untenanted in a yard knee-high with weeds. If anyone should come inquiring, though, the nets will be returned. More likely, each of us will be setting them, cleaned and sweet, to fill our own larders.

The case of these untended nets illustrates a general dilemma. We have three choices: looking on and twiddling our thumbs, calling the appropriate representative of law and order, or handling the matter ourselves. In regard to the nets, the first course scants justice altogether, with dreadful consequences for the fish but none at all for the person who slaughters and wastes them. The other choices offer satisfaction: an end to killing and a penalty imposed upon the killer. Why then, with public remedies at hand, do we more often choose to act privately as judge and jury? Frontier justice classically rectifies wrong by committing its own wrongs. Our retrieval of the careless nets could be construed as grand larceny; unless he comes inquiring, the owner is close to a thousand dollars out of pocket. One answer is that river people align themselves first on the side of the fish, rules and culprits be damned. A second is that Fisheries and Wildlife are understaffed and hard to reach; a call would bring action, but not before more fish had died. The most basic answer may be that the Point relishes independence and thrives on the immediate and ad hoc righting of a wrong. Besides, there's fun in cocking a snook at authority, in getting there first—as long as right is felt to outweigh wrong. Though we have flouted the law, we have honored ethics. The white boat with the blue motor has not yet reappeared.

Poaching is another kettle of fish or, more accurately, pot of crabs. Despite suspicions that erupt like thunder—"That SOB is reaming me!"—when a private boat pauses to pull up and inspect somebody else's private net, the dwellers at the Point are not wont to steal another's catch of fish. Such net-inspection stems from curiosity, not greed. Truly lawless attentions focus on one species of marine life, the blue crab. The commercial crabmen who give us waterfront seats for what we call "river TV" shows featuring theft and consequences.

The crabber in the hard-used boat with a blue stripe works an inshore line of crabpots set about thirty yards apart, each marked with a rectangular styrofoam float. He stands amidships, putting on speed between floats, then slowing, circling to catch each line connecting float to pot. Rhythmically, methodically, he labors: pull pot, empty catch, rebait pot, and drop it. Between our chores in the yard, we've watched him off and on for an hour. Suddenly, he's not alone. Like John Wayne riding down the gang that robbed the westbound stage, a red boat has roared out of one of the creeks that feed the Rounding—the red boat that usually fishes this inshore line. The shouting starts. Words slap the water, and water amplifies some well enough for us to hear. They're not worth hearing. The cause of the dispute is clear: who owns these crabs, the one who harvested or the one who expected to do the harvesting? The argument slams on till red boat fires a shot into the air. Blue-stripe hastily transfers the catch to red boat's waiting boxes. And red boat revs up, roars for port, while blue-stripe heads back downriver steering clear of every float, rectangular or not. The good guy wins. We're pleased, for we know that the crabber's life is not easy, hauling and resetting hundreds of pots daily, no matter that the heat may be hellish or the rain comes pelting. And for the tedium, the weariness, the vagaries of weather, the crabman

51

is a sharecropper. Working usually on contract to a buyer who furnishes the pots, he's paid according to his catch, the price of which fluctuates from barely adequate to downright poor, as the market dictates. The commercial poaching show, same plot with different casts, is scheduled for several re-runs every summer.

For another form of crab-poaching the miscreants are far less likely to be apprehended, cussed, and made to deliver stolen goods. It's poaching meant to appease the sneaky craving brought on by the approach of suppertime. When the wind blows out of the southwest and the river's depth at the crabline nearest shore is chest-high at most, some river-dwellers wade out and drag crabpots back ashore. The pots may or may not be returned after their contents are cooked and devoured. The young 'uns most often perpetrate this stunt, and several years ago, Al and Bonnie's middle daughter K.D., caught with hands on pot, was given permission to empty a pot or two as long as she rebaited them and put them back in place. Fair terms: nobody loses, not crabman nor child.

More often, however, children and adults, too, succumb more carelessly to temptation. Both crabs and pots are brought ashore, with the latter kept for personal use or simply tossed onto a rusting, weed-entangled heap of pots robbed earlier. Visitors may be most prone of all to take blue crabs they have not earned, especially visitors from inland who have despaired at the premium prices commanded by sea-food-market crustaceans not nearly so fresh as those that scuttle in the pots. I have seen one of our visitors, an inland man who lost a leg to military service, so overcome by blue-crab hunger that he planned well ahead of time to help himself. "I came prepared," he said, waving a spare prosthesis. "Don't matter if this ole leg do get all wet and fall apart. I'm gonna have me some *crab*." With a zesty limp and a slowly disintegrating artificial ankle, that's just what he did do, seizing three pots and pulling all three ashore at once. Wrong but, for him, somehow right. We set the pots back in place.

But what if someone takes a notion to steal from us? To pilfer the two-by-eights in a stack of lumber meant for pier-rebuilding? To break, enter, and trash a home?

Rumor has long held that the sheriff's men do not visit the Point because they shy away from driving their brown, star-emblazoned cars through the rough, tough community of nether Harlowe. On the first few miles of Adams Creek Road, rumor says, the makers of moonshine are fierce to defend their stills and will overturn a lawman's vehicle faster than white lightning can slide down a gullet. I've heard that on nights when 'shine is being sent on its potent journey through the copper coils, bicycle-mounted outriders pedal slowly up and down Adams Creek Road to utter warnings if the cops appear.

The sheriff's men are rarely seen in our back of beyond, though fear of revenue-evaders is not the reason. Nor is it, as some say, that deputies lose their bearings as they try to find us in this maze of backroads. In my second summer on the river, several residents circulated a petition calling for weekly patrols. Signatures, the Chief's and mine among them, filled the page. The petition was duly presented to the sheriff's office and agreed to, but men in uniforms and ranger hats did not noticeably increase their visibility. The truth about the absence of police is that the seven to ten patrol cars available at any one time cannot possibly maintain surveillance on every byway in a large, mostly rural county. As is, each car logs 110,000 miles a year. But deputies are far more readily contacted than game wardens. When summoned, they do come willingly to investigate the disappearance of a two-by-eight or a television set and to catch the occasional malefactor. But they cannot halt an incident before it occurs.

Preventative policework is up to us. One defense is a

simulacrum of community organization; its most apparent—
its only—gesture has been the posting of small Citizens
Watch signs. Policing the Point may take eccentric and aberrant forms, such as that favored by Jake, who has appointed
himself the local vigilante and guerrilla. When a vehicle he
does not recognize pulls into a nearby yard, he puts on fatigues left over from his military days, takes his twelve-gauge,
and crawls on his belly through tick- and chigger-infested
weeds to rise roaring under the nose of a terrified innocent,
sometimes the hapless householder arriving home in a bor-
rowed car. This much can be said for Jake in these forays: he's
not yet mistaken a person for a dog and pulled the trigger.
The Point's usual approach to unfamiliar vehicles and pedes-
trians—and we do watch for them—is mild: an unconcealed
advance, a "Howdy," and a calmly conversational inquiry
into the stranger's business. Mostly, it's innocuous: a real-
estate person looking over a newly listed property, a hunter
searching for a lost hound, an out-of-towner who camped
here as a kid, a group of missionaries well armed with tracts.
(I cannot figure out how missionaries find their way to the
river when rescue squads can't.) Once, when my daughter
came with friends to use the trailer in our absence, four people made four separate excursions to check on the legitimacy
of her presence.

The Point recently acquired a deputy of its own, a man
who works part-time for the sheriff's department. He moved
here not long ago with two string-bean teen-aged sons and a
lusty wife who uses her shotgun to keep their freezer well
stocked with venison. His roots in the general area reach back
some forty years; as the son of a commercial fisherman, he
was born to the water in a maritime community just south of
here—"Born," his wife vows, "with webs between his toes."
His daddy became a minister and in the '50s preached the
sermons at Oak Grove Church on the river road. We never
see our resident deputy in his official get-up, nor does he
bring his job home. Here, he's a true river rat. His boat trailer,

towed from home to various ramps down stretches of public road, bears no license tag. When it comes to crime, people who live on river time specialize for the most part in just such peccadillos.

Finally, Tom says, "I've got it now. You know, like cows and bulls, mares and stallions, bears come in sows and boars. A hogbear is nothing but a male black bear."

Well, yes! And we do see them occasionally. The Point is cornucopious with animals, not only white-tail deer and black bear, but 'possums and grey squirrels, river otters, bobcat, raccoons that swim the creek and have been known to climb at night through open windows to raid Bonnie's kitchen. And several people have spotted painters—mountain lions—at the edge of the dawn woods; just this summer one woman who knows her wildlife saw two young ones together, grey and unmistakably feline. What we don't see or catch a whiff of is polecats. Go twenty miles, however, and they're plentiful.

No sign will ever proclaim it, nor have I heard anyone use the term, but Great Neck Pointers have constituted themselves into a River Watch. Unlike Citizens Watch, it's not a matter that's been given conscious thought, nor is it so idle. As a matter of course, we keep a constant eye on water and earth, on weather and human damn-foolishness. Though water's cleanliness, the cool green shade of the woods, and the health of all creatures therein are of paramount importance, the thrust for river-watching arises not from some environmental passion but springs, sensible or lunatic, from the same protective instincts and self-interest that prompt homegrown responses to the need for law and order.

Al takes off his baseball cap, the one that reads "American by birth, Southern by choice," and scratches his head. (He's fond of caps with slogans; another one reads, "If you can't run with the big dogs, stay on the porch.") He glances back upriver at the path he's just taken, an invisible path through the water at river's edge. His old leather workboots, worn to protect feet from river trash, squish water as he shifts his weight. With an eye out for items to salvage, he's been exploring as far as the creek to check out the damage done by the rainless nor'easter that howled at nearly gale force all day yesterday and through the night. Today the winds blow fair out of the southwest.

"We-ell, she was a doozy, that storm. Looks like your neighbor lost himself another foot of land," he says and pulls the fruits of beachcombing from his jacket pockets—a still bright fishing lure, old floats made of real cork not plastic, and an inkwell of the sort used years ago in schoolrooms. These inkwells, from the old one-room elementary schools on the peninsula, are a frequent find.

The Nay-Sayer's property immediately upriver from ours grows smaller with each storm, receding as much as ten feet inland a year as the wind-pushed river chews it up and spits it toward the sea. The Chief remembers the property's extent in 1965 when he first saw Great Neck Point. Its grassy lawn, a clearing in the woods, reached much farther into the river than did the lot we now live on, and a pier connected to shore extended the land's reach over the river. In 1979, when the Chief acquired our place, the land next door had been so eroded that its riverward margin matched ours. The Nay-Sayer bought it in 1980, and weeds began to usurp the lawn; vines grew exuberantly around, then into the old Spartan Mansion, an Airstream-type of trailer, parked in the woods-embraced clearing. Vandals broke into the Mansion stripping it and building fires on the kitchen counter. The pier was gone by then, its presence indicated only by isolated pilings tenanted by gulls and royal terns. But the concrete survey monument from the old farm's division into lots still stood beneath an aged sweetgum tree. When I arrived on the river, to that silent fanfare of dead ducks, monument and tree had both fallen into the water. Part of the tree is visible today; trunk and branches long gone, the upside-down stump remains, thrusting into air water-blackened roots where barnacles nest. The Chief showed me photographs of the monument topped with red paint and snugged in the grassy earth near the base of the tree. I never expected to see its concrete reality.

Every four or five years, wind demonstrates its unstoppable force not by driving hungry waves onto land but by bulldozing the water far offshore. The phenomenon occurs when wind hauls from its customary southwest or northeast quarters and comes hard and steady out of the southeast. "A leaning wind," I call it, for a human being can stand relaxed against it yet be supported almost upright by its blast. Under this push, the river retreats twenty-five to fifty yards, leaving its bed, here sand, there clay, exposed directly to the light and air. Stripped of its liquid counterpane, the bed is seen to be full of crumbs. And people will take a day off from work to do housekeeping chores in their normally drowned front yards. They lug away crumbling cinderblocks, bald tires, and sodden timbers, all colonized by barnacles, mussels, and oysters that snag gill nets. They load five-gallon buckets with toe-stubbing bricks, toe-knifing aluminum pop-tops, and countless shards of varicolored glass. They pick up old soda and beer cans, half-rusted testimony to the durability of steel. Sometimes a trophy is found, a ballast stone dropped who knows when by a sailing ship or a bottle made of pressed glass. Dorothy has found another, older kind of glass on the shore of the Nay-Sayer's property: the thick, square bottoms of the handblown bottles in which the early wooden vessels carried potables for consumption on board. In his kitchen, Al displays a younger bottle he found some years ago. It is unchipped and barely abraded by sand. The word *Pep-Tone* is molded in the clear glass. The Pep-Tone Company, long defunct, tried for the success of its cola-concoction by half-echoing the name of Pepsi. The beverage failed, but the bottle is a minor collector's item.

On just such a clean-swept, southeast day in 1984, Al found the vanished monument and summoned us. It lay on the sand five yards from the riverbank. Its four-sided, pyramidal top still showed traces of red paint. Al and the Chief measured off its distance from shore and our bulkhead. Water-action seemed not to have moved this heavy object significantly far from the coordinates that once marked its place on land. The Chief circled it, taking photos, and then snapped a shot of me leaning on the wind.

In the few years since the discovery of the monument's watery grave, the Nay-Sayer's unprotected property has receded still farther inland. We look at the pilings of the old pier—only three are standing now, not yet brought low by storms and wood-boring worms, and we see that erosion has eaten back the land a good eighty feet along the 150-foot stretch of riverfront immediately adjacent to our lot. The land that once reached farther than ours into the river now lies more than fifty feet inland of our riverfront. Letting the land go seems a vandalism far worse than that wreaked in the old Spartan Mansion.

Not long after the property acquired its present absentee owner, one gesture was made to hinder such loss. Not to stop it, for no bulkhead was built nor a permit to build one ever applied for. Instead, chunky rectangles of still mortared bricks and several dozen hedgehogs—heavy, tapered blocks of poured concrete used for anchoring fences—were dumped on the land at river's edge. Like the sweetgum and the survey monument, they have plopped into the river where it was hoped they'd act as revetments. The river ignores this rubble. Some of it now rests underwater yards from shore. Blue crabs play in the ruins. Inshore, on the tops of still exposed hedgehogs, water moccasins bask in the sun.

The state estimates the average rate of erosion for both shores of the lower Neuse at two feet a year. Such erosion, erasing many of the long strips of sandy beach that bordered the river only a decade ago, is due primarily to a recent and documented increase in the rate at which sea level is rising. But two feet can turn easily into ten a year if the storms blow severe. The continuing loss next door could eat away our land

58

and turn us into an island if we let it. We have countered by adding, first, a fifty-foot wing-wall to our bulkhead and, later, extending the wall another twenty-five feet. The wing-wall, constructed like the bulkhead of lumber treated to resist marine organisms, makes a right angle inland at the upriver corner of our lot. Only the last five yards are still buried under the soil. The Nay-Sayer has put his property up for sale. We hope for a buyer who believes in bulkheads and has the means to construct one. The cost will be in the upper tens of thousands. I hope, too, for someone who believes in preserving the warbler-seducing woods and the prickly pears lining the path to creek and pond, for someone who says a whole-hearted Yes to living on river time. But the land is so ravaged that it may be unsaleable.

River Watch stays on the lookout for another kind of erosion. Its overt symptom is fences—fences on the land, fences in the river, bold fences warning all comers not to trespass.

It may be simply ignorance that builds a barricade from shore well into the water. The river belongs to the public, no matter that we like to think of it as a submarine extension of our yards. North Carolina guarantees anyone access to the water; the ten feet of shore from mean water level is a promenade open alike to river-dweller, inlander, or visitor from a distant planet. The Point's residents build their share of ornamental fences—railings, mostly, of hand-split pine set in hand-hewn, hand-drilled cedar posts. One such beauty surrounds Al's vegetable patch; Dorothy's red trumpet honeysuckle, transplanted from the woods and savored by orchard orioles, clings to another. These enclosures are grace notes embellishing the landscape, and ten feet from the water they stop short, leaving unobstructed the public's right-of-way. A few landowners, though, shout discourteously to shoo the passer-by off "their" riverbanks, and a few go so far as to build fences that barge straight on to water's edge and then plunge in, sending chainlink tens of feet from shore and shamelessly announcing "Mine! Keep out!" To wade around

these barriers in daylight and slosh through "private" water
bears little risk except, perhaps, for bellowed rudeness from
the river's would-be proprietor. At night, when darkness
masks faces and forms, beware. Unwitting trespassers in
search of flounder have been shot at. River Watch spreads the
word.

On land the general scenario is this: a family living just
behind the tier of waterfront lots arrives home to find its yard
bisected by a line of stakes or, worse, chainlink fence erected
across the lawn. (Such stakes and fences seem to sprout when
no one is home, as if the perpetrator knows in the bone, if not
the brain, that planting new boundaries is neither ethical nor
legal.) Head of family explodes and pulls up the stakes or
goes off to borrow one of the Point's two tractors to tear the
offending chainlink out by its cement roots. The reason for
erecting stakes or fences holds no rationality, but it can take
time and nearly ruptured patience to persuade a fence-builder
that his efforts were out of line—and off the boundary line, as
well. The problem springs from a hard-headed misunder-
standing of the language in title deeds.

Many of the deeds for the Point's land are written in the
inexact terminology associated with pirates' treasure maps.
Boundaries are set by references to so-and-so's drainage ditch,
to the old cypress in the southwest corner of the pond, to the
center of Courts Creek. But so-and-so and his ditch are long
gone, the cypress has been felled by man or time, and the
creek may have wandered, slightly changing its course. The
old descriptions, however, rest on the page in tandem with
more modern references to metes and bounds—measure-
ments given in feet and inches and boundaries set in coordinates of longitude and latitude. It's the feet and inches that
send fence-builders into frenzies of encroachment. If a deed
specifies so many feet, then, to some minds, the figures are
immutable. Thus, if the river takes a dozen feet, a property
line is to be moved a dozen feet inland—right into someone
else's yard. But the encroached-upon are quick to reimpose

proper limits on both land and the land-grabber. If he's around, the grabber may reclaim his fence. If not, brand new but illicit chainlink with all the shiny fittings has a way of disappearing, leaving only paper remnants, checks or dollar bills, in the victim's hand.

We walk with Al to view the new land-losses next door. On calm days, the river tongues the clay bank like a child licking a lollipop. Under the fierce impetus of a nor'easter, the waves grow teeth, tearing at the clay. A trail of light brown mud discolors the dark water as it streams down the river's long gut to the sea. What the river has taken from the Nay-Sayer is gone not for good but forever. The land cannot be reclaimed.

Water, earth, the air that blows us gales or cools the hottest summer day—three of the elements anciently believed to form the universe are present always at the Point. The fourth, fire, may be invited and contained or may burst forth groping blindly for fodder and gorging itself on woods and fields, chattels and houses. If Al is at home, the first cry for help goes to him.

These days, if you ask an eight-year old boy what he wants to be when he grows up, he may well answer pilot or basketball player or MTV star. It used to be, however, that a good many small fry could be counted on to say, "A fireman!" Shaggy-browed Al, who is only months from his fiftieth birthday but looks and acts a decade younger, seems to exemplify that old-time little boy whose wish came true. Al's weekday occupation is that of senior sheet metal mechanic, aircraft, at Cherry Point where, since discharge from the Marines twenty-two years ago, he has disassembled, repaired, and refitted removable parts for such planes as Harriers, F-4 Phantom fighters, and the lumbering C-130s and C-131s that carry cargo. He's an expert at developing patterns where no sketches or samples exist. He's worked with almost every kind of ferrous and non-ferrous metals, including such exotics

61

as titanium. He's at ease with the immense and inherently dangerous machines that drill, grind, punch, cut, form, stretch, shrink, and coil metal. Naturally, he's button-bursting proud of what he does and can do. But at heart he's a fireman.

The official designation is firefighter. Al, Bonnie, and Kent represent the Point on the 26-member roster of the Harlowe Volunteer Fire Department, which Al joined two years ago. But his fire-battling days go farther back than that, for he was a charter member of the Havelock Fire Department, organized twenty years ago. The other members of the VFD, black and white, reside along Adams Creek Road and the other byways of the spread-out community that the Harlowe station serves. Bonnie, as a certified Emergency Medical Technician, acts as its one-woman rescue squad. (The full-time, regional rescue squad is based in Havelock and charges $65 for each call outside the city limits.) Every last person on the roster is strictly a volunteer, including the fire chief, a Harlowe man, who makes his living in Havelock as a barber. And everyone, to maintain active membership, is required by state law to put forty-two hours a year into training, not just in the art of dousing flames and treating victims of smoke inhalation but in the emergency services expected of fire departments—extracting the injured from auto smashes and helping babies into the world. I imagine that many of the volunteers have realized a half-formed childhood wish to be a fireman, but Al has gone them one better. Not only does he have the right to doff his slogan-shouting baseball cap and don a helmet, not only does a call-monitor connected to the station fill his house with a dispatcher's disembodied voice, but he has a real live fire truck parked mere feet from his back door.

It's a venerable truck, a high-snouted 1952 four-wheel-drive Ford fitted out as a pumper by American La France. The mars light sits like a revolving red jewel on the cab's brow. A 24-foot extension ladder hangs on the outside starboard wall of the truckbed; the port wall bears an axe and two stout black connection hoses with bright silver rings at both ends. In the truckbed, two reels above the 300-gallon water tank hold two hundred feet of flexible, smaller gauge hose. Little, weather-worn curlicue-decals ornament the fenders and truckbed walls. Newer, larger blazons, which are stylized black-on-silver representations of a helmet and other appurtenances of the firefighter's job, embellish the doors and proclaim the truck's affiliation—HARLOWE—in letters legible across a good-sized field. The emblem overlays an earlier set of stick-on letters now pulled off but still announcing through their adhesive remains that once the pumper belonged to the small town of Princeton, located a hundred miles inland amid to-bacco fields. Princeton bought the truck as salvage at an auction held by its original owner, the U. S. Air Force. The state inspection sticker on the pumper's windshield expired last year.

"But she works, oh yes, she works. She'll put out a fire before the new equipment gets this far," Al says in his broad-voweled Hoosier voice. He pats her flank.

She works because of his ministrations. Her hood is kept open a fraction of an inch so that the battery charger set atop the right fender can give on-going resuscitation. The charger is protected against rain by a five-gallon bucket that once held drywall joint compound. A large puddle lies perpetually be-neath the truck because the water tank long ago sprang a slow leak. Al tops the tank out daily. He's rearranged her gearing, too, so that when her engine must switch from propelling ve-hicle to pumping water, it will give willing cooperation rather than the flat-out refusal he encountered the first time he tried to activate the pump. Fondly, he refers to her as "my mon-ster." The truck belongs to the Harlowe VFD but, because of her super-annuated condition, it was decided that she could be put out to pasture at Great Neck Point. And to the Point she may mean the difference between staying green or going to blazes.

The volunteers have seen and fought fire in its most dramatic and devastating pyrophanies—the red crackling flames, their lion-like roar, the reek and skyward roll of black smoke, the timbers breaking and crashing, followed by sparks that spit like firecrackers. For those of us who are not firemen, it calls itself to our attention with quieter insistence. A dense and tawny cloud clings to the rivershore for three days and the resinous scent of cooking pines greases the air: forest fire. Or smoke rises southeast of the pond and spreads a grey pall over windy blue sky: trash fire out of control and burning the brushy fields. Fire comes with predictable irregularity and goes, leaving its signature of black, black ashes on the cleared land, the woods floor, and the heat-wrenched metal of mobile homes.

In the eye-blink of time that the river-washed Point has governed my wakings and my sleep, no major fires have come here. The fires I've seen have been amenable, contained, benign, except perhaps for the occasional incineration of old tires dragged from the river and stacked on the sandy beach near the creek. Drenched with kerosene, they ignite readily and blaze and melt, staining the air with thick, oily smoke and a chemical stench. These summer-night conflagrations seem to be a form of pyromaniacal thumb-twiddling indulged in by kids too long out of school. Our usual fires are the campfires that Al and Bonnie's middle daughter K.D. makes, to cook stone soup in an iron kettle hung from a tripod in her back yard. Or the bonfires we build winter and summer of dead-wood at river's edge and light just after dark on a calm night—marshmallow-toasting fires once they reduce themselves to embers. Or the coals that the Chief creates from pine-cone-kindled cedar to brown pork chops or barbecue filleted but unscaled mullet on our outdoor grill. Vigilance is kept over these small fires, and if one should spark out of bounds or the wind rise, we smother incipient disaster with a blanket or drown it with a well-aimed hose.

But if lightning should strike out of stormy air—or aged

64

wiring or human carelessness, Al's worthy but dilapidated lady might not suffice to stay the flames. She's a stopgap, just enough to wet the leading edge of a brushfire before the volunteers assemble and more up-to-date equipment makes its way down slow-speed miles of curving road. In case of major fires, those thirteen miles could be a hundred.

In makeshift, can-do, forty-five MPH fashion, the Point for the most part efficiently protects itself. The open secret is devout observance of the commandment to be neighborly. And, in a corollary, those who live here tolerate a high degree of quirkiness and welcome any visitor, any would-be resident who demonstrates a gut-regard for the unwritten rules. Such people have never been strangers here. But sometimes others who are eternal aliens stumble on the Point and stumble into things they have not reckoned with.

After the event I look at the watch that still manacles my wrist and discover that it's four AM. It's the hour that most perturbs insomniacs,. the hour most appointed for dying. As the event begins, I am waked by a dim awareness that my husband is out of bed and groping for something in the dark. It takes a moment before I hear what he's already heard—pounding, pounding, pounding at the front door. Sal barks. The pounding does not relent.

Good Lord, it's Tom and Merle. Her mother's been sick. They have no phone. They want to use ours.

The Chief is still groping, turns out he's trying to find his jeans. I pull on a robe.

It can't be Merle and Tom. They'd bang on the bedroom wall and call our names.

A young woman, dark-haired, big-eyed, stands clad in tank top, shorts, and sneakers at the door. "C'n I use your phone?"

Something about her cancels any impulse toward hospitality. "Absolutely not."

"But we're lost!"

I step out onto the deck. She wants to call the police, the fire department, the rescue squad, the Coast Guard, any agency at all to take her home. What's the cause of this distress? It takes a long, shadowy while to find out. As the Chief, who's finally found his mislaid jeans, joins me, a blond man, barechested and bespectacled, materializes out of the darkness. As the woman wails that she must get home, the man tells us as best he can what's happened. Yesterday afternoon, the twosome launched an outboard motor boat from a public ramp some three miles upriver, crossed the water to the far shore, and started on the return voyage after dark. Disoriented, they'd run out of gas and beached the boat hours ago at a place with a two-story house and a concrete boat ramp. No one was home. A house and private ramp—clues enough to let us know that they'd come ashore a mile upriver from our place. That house sits lonely in a wilderness, no other human habitations for a mile on either side, and though the shore offers a few smooth stretches of sandy beach, much of it is an obstacle course. Impelled by night-bred terrors, the woman has broken the cardinal rule of castaways: Stay by your boat till daylight comes. She has been pulled downriver by the brightness of the two security lights in our yard. To reach us, she has fled through tree roots and stumps, through barnacled snags and submerged pilings, through debris bristling with knife-sharp oyster shells. Unable to divert her, the man has followed.

We explain that, lacking an emergency, no fireman nor law-enforcement officer, no ambulance nor Coast Guard craft will speed to rescue someone merely lost.

"These people are right," the man says to her.

"I have to go to work," she wails. "I'll walk to the road. I'll get a lift."

We tell her that the main road is twelve miles distant. She doesn't believe us. The man asks if they may wait in our yard till daylight. Of course. He settles himself into a lawn chair. She, however, stalks off, heading back upriver and howling, "I left my two kids alone at home!" After several minutes, he rises and trudges after her.

We return to bed, and a light, giveaway snore announces that the Chief has also returned to his dreams. Behind closed eyes, I lie awake chastising myself for lack of charity and congratulating myself for having kept hysteria outside the door. If only we had mentioned water moccasins and rattlesnakes and drowning, if only we had tied her to a tree, if only I'd remembered how to shock a person back to rationality and slapped her hard across her face. . . . If only she had mentioned those two children first off, my own motherhood would have opened the door wide so that she could check on their welfare. There are indeed strange, skulking creatures here at Great Neck Point, and I'm one of them.

But in the daylight we tell the tale of our unexpected visitors. No one at the Point, no one at all, would have opened the door. Dorothy shudders and tells us that we have lived out her long-held nightmare of invasive strangers breaking down a darkened door. In the minds of our friends, we have not broken the commandment to be neighborly. It is the strangers who have violated the second prime injunction by failing to respect the river. Al says it aloud: "Stupid! Don't they realize the river can kill?"

Living peaceably on our frontier, we call little attention to ourselves. And we live with the river day and night. No matter what our preoccupations, it flows through all we do and are. We know it hides its own sorts of demons. But there's a dark side to our knowledge and our habit of lying low: in times of crisis, the Point's ability to serve a greater cause may well be overlooked.

Al, sweaty from tilling his garden, looks at the float plane droning slowly overhead. The sun, nearly down, has turned the choppy water crimson. He says, "It's hopeless now. If they had called us first, we could have helped."

Not many days ago, in the late afternoon, three people

from the next county—a man, his 22-year-old son, and the son's three-year-old boy—went fishing. They launched a flat-bottomed, sixteen-foot aluminum johnboat from the same public ramp that our four-AM strangers did. At 8:55 PM, several hours after the time they'd stipulated for their return, the authorities were notified and the search began. Three counties have sent rescue-squad boats manned by volunteers; the boats have been cruising the Rounding and the river proper. Sometimes they've hugged the shore, a man in his squad's uniform standing in the stern with hand on tiller while a barelegged spotter sits astride the bow, binoculars scanning the undersides of the Point's piers and the jutting, snarly roots of trees undermined by erosion. The Wildlife Commission has also sent in small craft. From two separate stations, the Coast Guard has mounted patrols on water and in the air: a brightly orange, rigid-hull inflatable boat and a white helicopter decorated with blue and red slash-stripes. From Cherry Point, the Marines have dispatched Pedro, the H-46 Search-and-Rescue helicopter; it whirrs, hovers, and whirrs on again. The Fisheries float plane flies low searching, searching, searching, and the Civil Air Patrol has joined the crowd aloft. On the water private boats swarm in, weaving their courses amid the crabpot markers, while the crabmen go about their business as usual and keep an eye out for the unusual. For days, starting the afternoon the johnboat was put in the water, the winds have gusted hard and rain has fallen intermittently on waves that wear white beards. The chop on the water is one of the roughest we've seen. The watching Point knows that in this weather anyone familiar with the river would not have launched a frail craft.

The morning after the boat was reported missing, the older man was found alive atop the overturned hull, which had been held at the point of capsize by its anchor. All night the remorseless water had slammed him against the aluminum, and he said that he felt as if he'd been beaten by a baseball bat. Suffering from hypothermia, he was taken to the hospital and assured recovery. Earlier that morning, the child had been found miles away on the river's far shore drowned and wearing a small life jacket to which a man-sized jacket had been tied. It is the child's young father for whom this populous and costly search has been mounted.

The county's director of Emergency Medical Services, who is also New Bern's fire chief, pits human resources against the wind and rain. The wind drives like a battering fist, coming now from the northwest, now from the northeast. The waves rise high, bubble, and break; foam lathers the water. A rescue squad member says, "The water is so rough it's hard to see anything." The weather's unfriendliness to small craft is not the only obstacle: the searchers face the needle-in-a-haystack problem of not knowing quite where, in these miles of river, the grey and heaving megatons of water may have shoved anything as insubstantial as flesh and bone. The director says, "We just don't have an area that we can pin down. But we'll continue searching as long as we feel we can find something."

"Too late," Al says. "All those people looking, all those boats and planes—a lot of work and money. For what? If they'd only let us down here know as soon as the boat was reported missing, we could have gone out. We know the river, we have the boats for rough weather, we've got people trained for emergencies. We might have found the baby and his dad, not alive maybe, but found 'em."

On the sixth day, the sky begins to clear, the wind to slacken. The director of Emergency Medical Services says, "As the weather gets better and more people are out on the river, it's possible that we may find him or that someone else might find him by accident. It's up to the laws of nature at this point." The wind still snorts and paws at the water, but the river has calmed enough for fishing. Most of the Point's gill nets, however, stay dry. Not given to worst-case scenarios, the Chief and I do set our net and harvest blues and spot and trout.

By the morning of the tenth day, crews still crowd the water and the sky. The sounds of search become sounds given voice and body by a tribe that has not repressed the ancient art of lamentation—random cries, the throaty hum of motors, the float plane's engine droning a slow dirge, the helicopter rotors beating air like hands thumping on a breast. We at the Point defend ourselves from the intolerable by absorbing the sounds as people who live in cities absorb and cease to hear the fire engines and the sirens that scream reminders of mortality. By the evening of the eleventh day, the river again sports its usual complement of corklines and paired yellow floats.

It seems likely now that there's nothing to be found. Our part-time deputy, who has participated actively in the search, says, "We've got to make sure. That's the way we do things here."

On the eighteenth day, the young man is found in a marsh two miles from the site of capsize. Discovery is accidental. Not a search party, but dogs out for a run find and lead their master to his few remains. A scrap of his corduroy pants and a pocket knife serve to identify him. The boats depart. The float plane circles one last time, banks, and turns for home.

4

The Truth about Yesterday

‖ LOOK AT ALMOST the same landscape, almost the same kind
of water that the Indians and later colonists saw, that existed
here long before there were men to set eyes on them. The
river began nearly two million years ago in the early
Pleistocene, as a gift from the mountains. Springs welling in
the Appalachians and rains falling on those heights coalesced,
gathered strength, and sought the sea—a little, nameless river
carving the course that its successors will follow. It was the
melting of the glaciers fifteen thousand years ago, and the
consequent rise in sea level that made the river fat and wide.
The soil of the coastal plain is sediment, sand and clay,
washed down anciently and now from the mountains. It
grows no rocks, and if we find a stone, any stone at all, we
know that it was brought here by human agency: mortars for
grinding corn, flint arrowheads, the granite ballast stones
dropped by the wooden ships when they took on the weight
of cargo, and the grey, fossil-bearing marl that we have lately
imported to give firmness to the Point's dirt lanes. As earth's
great geologic changes may be read in layered rock, so may

71

the changes wrought by people on the lower river be read in stones.

The trees and vines and shrubs that I see amid the timber company's pines on this uninhabited shore were here to greet the Indians. They looked on the eternal pines, sweetgums, and red cedars, the live oaks wearing beards of Spanish moss, the short-lived water oaks with dead limbs in which the red-bellied woodpeckers nest, the black gums—actually tupelos—that were believed to be the only trees immune to being split and toppled by lightning. With fire and tools of stone and bone, the Indians hollowed the trunks of baldy cypress for their canoes. In mid-spring, the rich fragrance of yellow jessamin reached their noses, and at spring's end, the equally heady scent of honeysuckle. Their tongues surely tasted the bay-leaf flavor of myrtle in their soups and stews. Their stomachs surely felt the blow dealt by *Ilex vomitoria*, the yaupon holly that grows liberally in shady places, that the Chief has transplanted from the woods to ornament the earth beside our deck. The young holly leaves were dried and steeped to make a caffeinaceous tea. For special occasions the berries were added to the brew. Their effect is that explicitly described by the species name; such potent drink was used in religious ceremonies as a purgative.

The birds they saw here are those the Chief promised me and all the others I have spotted since and some that no longer throng on this coast, the wild turkeys and the great flocks of parakeets. The same otters play in the water, the same hogbears root in the forests, the same bobcats scream at daybreak, the same mountain lions walk like grey shadows at the edge of the woods. As for the fish, most species perdure, though some may now be vanished, such as the sturgeon seven feet long with bony scale-plates that could be used as graters. The Indians were bitten by the very pests that gorge on us, the red bugs that keep me itching summer-long, the golden-eyed deerflies, the gnats, mosquitoes and ticks. The Indians reached for repellent as quickly as we do, smearing their bodies with ripe animal fat. And they walked as warily as we lest snakes be startled and attack.

Fear, delight, amazement—with all my feelings, all my senses, I experience the physical reality of the Paradise called Great Neck Point. But I can only imagine the Indians through what they've left behind. Long before, but not long after, the coming of Europeans, distinct groups of Indians occupied or ranged this coast. Tribal names cannot be fixed upon the early groups, but they can be generally distinguished now as speakers of Algonquian, Iroquoian, or Siouan languages. It may be that the groups were not entirely tribal but aggregations joined by kinship, trade ties, or seasonal hunting needs into bands that travelled loosely bounded and large territories. In slow stages they began to arrive here perhaps ten thousand years ago as hunter-gatherers pursuing game, picking wild plant-foods, and fishing the river. With the advent of agriculture about a thousand years before the coming of the colonists, they adopted slash-and-burn methods that saw villages erected temporarily amid newly created fields that would be cultivated till fertility ran out and it was time to move on to nearby virgin land. Nor did they depend solely upon domestic crops but hunted and fished for their proteins and collected natural plantfoods as assiduously as ever. The European adventurers of the late sixteenth century provided the first specific information about discrete coastal tribes—the Secotan on the north shore of the Pamlico River, the Pomouik of what is now Pamptico-Pamplico-Pamlico County, the Coree with a base near the present site of Beaufort on Bogue Sound, the incursive and combative Tuscarora building a stronghold near present New Bern, the Neusiok—or Neiosioke, as they were first called in English—presiding on our shore in the area encompassing the Point. Of their presence, little now remains except their unintended gifts—a word here, a vegetable there. The squash, melons, corn, and beans that we harvest abundantly were developed from the native North American plants that the Indians cultivated. From them also came tobacco, then an item for ceremonial and religious use, now the curse-and-blessing that keeps a lot of North Carolinians off the unemployment rolls. The languages of the coastal peoples are almost as vanished as the peoples themselves, their words and names now serving mainly as geographical designations—Hatteras, Roanoke, the much transformed Pamlico. The Neusiok were never a large nation; the colonial census of 1700 enumerated them at a mere thousand. Soon thereafter, smallpox wiped them out.

What the Neusiok called the river by which they lived is not recorded. If the Tuscarora had prevailed here, the river might have been given the name they used—Cautonah, Pine-in-Water. Or it might have been Wee quo Whom, as a tribe by the falls on the upper river referred to it. It was an Englishman, Arthur Barlowe, who gave sanction in 1584 to the name Neuse. Captain of a pinnace not much bigger than a long-boat, he was second-in-command of the exploratory expedition sent westward by Sir Walter Raleigh to survey the possibilities for seating a colony on the North Carolina coast. Barlowe took back precisely the glowing account that Sir Walter desired in order to get Queen Elizabeth's royal go-ahead for such a project. The result: the Roanoke Colony, Virginia Dare, and the disappearance of both into history's erasures. In his propaganda, Barlowe mentioned the "Countrey Neiosioke, situate upon the side of a goodly River called Neus." And so it has been known ever since.

The goodly River flows still through territory that a slightly later propagandist called the "delicious Country," the "Summer-Country." These phrases are those of John Lawson, widely travelled Surveyor General to the British Lords Proprietors of North Carolina. In his 1709 prospectus *A New Voyage to Carolina*, he described the milk-and-honey land that met his gaze and wrote of planters:

 . . . finding mild Winters, and a fertile Soil, beyond
Expectation, producing every thing that was planted, to a
prodigious Increase; their Cattle, Horses, Sheep, and

74

Swine, breeding very fast, and passing the Winter without any Assistance from the Planter; so that every thing seem'd to come by Nature, the Husbandman living almost void of Care, and free from those Fatigues which are absolutely requisite in Winter-Countries, for providing Fodder and other Necessaries; these Encouragements induc'd them to stand their Ground, altho' but a handful of People, seated at great Distances one from another, and amidst a vast number of *Indians* of different Nations, who were then in *Carolina*. Nevertheless, I say, the Fame of this new-discover'd Summer-Country spread through the neighbouring Colonies, and in a few Years, drew a considerable Number of Families thereto, who all found Land enough to settle themselves in, (had they been many Thousands more) and that which was very good and commodiously seated, both for Profit and Pleasure. And, indeed, most of the Plantations in *Carolina* naturally enjoy a noble Prospect of large and spacious Rivers, pleasant Savanna's, and fine Meadows, with their green Liveries, interwoven with beautiful Flowers, of most glorious Colours, which the several Seasons afford; hedg'd in pleasant Groves of the ever-famous Tulip-tree, the stately Laurel, and Bays, equalizing the Oak in Bigness and Growth; Myrtles, Jessamines, Wood-bines, Honeysuckles, and several other fragrant Vines and Ever-greens, whose aspiring Branches shadow and interweave themselves with the loftiest Timbers, yielding a pleasant Prospect, Shade and Smell, proper habitations for the Sweet-singing Birds, that melodiously entertain such as travel thro' the Woods of *Carolina*.

Beulah Land, Utopia, in truth an earthly Paradise—John Lawson understood the art of hyperbole as well as any real-estate pitchman wooing a prospect. Note that he did not forget to mention the Profit, as well as the Pleasure, to be obtained from such a land. His blandishments certainly lured more than a few settlers to the town of New Bern, which he helped found, surveying its land into lots and streets as tidy as those of the modern-day planned communities that dimple the river's wooded banks on New Bern's outskirts.

He also had an ardent, almost omnivorous curiosity that led him to identify, list, and describe every plant and animal that he found in Summer-Country. His lists could be taken as a guide by anyone who wished not to live as an industrious planter-ant but as a grasshopper plucking whatever was at hand and putting nothing by. One could hunt for bear, the flesh of which was "nourishing and not inferior to the best Pork in Taste" and for lark-sized Sand-Birds—probably plover or sandpipers—"a dainty Food, if you will bestow Time and Ammunition to kill them." There were fruits to be gathered, berries, nuts, persimmons, and fox grapes. And the water's bounty had no end: Blue Fish, Crocus (as he called croaker), Mullets, all the other swimmers that leap now into our nets, and Eels "no where in the World better, or more plentiful than in *Carolina*."

John Lawson and other contemporary observers didn't always know what species they were looking at and reached home to England for an analogy and a name. As a result, some fish entirely native to American waters often bear the British names of unrelated but look-alike species, names bestowed by colonists three hundred years ago: chub for large-mouthed bass, roach for the golden shiner, jack pike for chain pickerel.

John Lawson's journals, lists, and gung-ho enticements found publication and, thus, preservation just in time. In 1711, two years after his book of lauds appeared, he was made prisoner and killed by the Tuscarora.

Great Neck Point has its share of ghosts. They haunt us through the pleasure of finding their artifacts, the potsherds and arrowheads and broken bottles with pontil marks. Or, when the weather lowers and the river rises, they stir in us a sense of respectful unease. But one ghost is a daily presence at the Point, benign as a glass calm on a summer day or malevolent as a February nor'easter, depending on how the person speaking of her knew her.

Joyce says, "When Mo and I first met Miss Carrie—that was 1967—it was a hot day in August. Gol*lee*, it was hot. She had on a clean housedress, and she was wearing hose. A lady, always a lady, so sweet and precise."

Miss Carrie was born to the Point, though her actual birthplace was on the river's far shore in Pamlico County—or Pamplico or Pamptico, again depending on the person speaking, for the antique pronunciations spelled out on colonial maps are still used in these rural parts. Her parents, John and Mary Grover, owned and farmed this land and here built the house where she played as a child with her two sisters.

The land and the woods, not the river and commercial fishing, provided the Point's daily bread from the 1880s well past World War II. The Grovers' farm, accessible like the other farms on the peninsula only by a dirt wagon track, sprawled along the shore. In the manner of country places, it was self-sufficient. John Grover not only farmed but operated a forge near the junction of the river and Courts Creek. The forge has left no traces, and a collector dredged water-covered sand some years ago and took away all the rusted wrought iron he could find, but John Grover's reputation as a master wheelwright remains. His crops were carted, most likely in wagons with iron tires of his own making, to a farmers' market on the Point's downriver end, and there they were loaded aboard boats for freighting upriver to the flourishing port of New Bern. Some of the boats may have been hauled and repaired here on the now-vanished marine railway at the mouth of Courts Creek.

Boats also transported timber from the woodlands surrounding the farms by towing it in great log-rafts to New Bern's lumber mills. Some trees, however, never left home before they were processed into the multiple products that pines can yield. An immemorially ancient method of extracting pine tar was used well into John Grover's day—tar kettles, evidence of which can still be seen in the forests on the peninsula. Two are situated in the woods behind Mo and Joyce's house—large, circular depressions in the earth that are encompassed by a deeper trench. Cut pines were piled in these depressions and set afire; as they burned, the sap bubbled dark and viscous into the trenches and was collected for rendering into tar and pitch, essential stores for caulking wooden ships. Pines were also tapped for oils that could be distilled into turpentine and rosin. Sawmills were constructed in the woods and fields. One of them, Winthrop Mills, became the focus and support of an ad hoc town. Built near the turn of the century on cleared land near the corner where the VFD substation will soon rise, it converted raw pines into every possible product from oils to boards. The Mill laid a cog railway so that its goods could go creaking and clattering from the peninsula to market. The last road in to the Point crosses a hollow that contains a portion of the old track. Ed and Beulah's sons, when they were adolescent, used to go there hunting snakes.

Born to the Point, Miss Carrie stayed on the Point and settled into it for the rest of her long life. She married Cap'n Charlie, also born in Pamlico (or Pamplico or Pamptico). The turn-off road to the Point is named for him in the fashion that many of the one-time farm-to-market tracks off Adams Creek Road were named—for the proprietors of the land at their termini. Cap'n Charlie—it's said that he was a big person, tall and lanky, who looked like a seafaring man though he farmed all his life. The Cap'n is a honorific bestowed, as Kentucky bestows the rank of Colonel, on a leading citizen. Not many people now alive recall him in his vigor; most of our neighbors knew him just to look at. He was old then and had long been sick, spending his days in a rocking chair and nodding greetings to passers-by. His granddaughter Eva describes him as "a good-natured man, but he didn't take no nonsense." I see him as laconic, not much given to disputation but diligent

78

at farming the acres that his wife inherited. Tiny Miss Carrie anyhow had sugar and spice, piss and vinegar enough for two.

"*Always* a lady," Joyce says.

"And probably quite a girl," Mo adds. "She told me she met Cap'n Charlie when she was eleven but waited till she was thirteen to marry him."

And Rita Fay, youngest of her many granddaughters, says, "Our granddaddy Charlie—he lived to be eighty-six—was fourteen years older than her. He asked her to marry him when they were riding home from church in a horse-drawn cart."

In eight pregnancies, Miss Carrie bore him nine children, three of whom—Claude, Sheldon, and Lena—survived to adulthood. She outlived these three and several grandchildren as well, and she outlived farming as the Point's prime means of making a livelihood, though bright-leaf tobacco was still being topped and cropped, cured and sent off to market till 1976, the year before her death.

The tobacco barn that Cap'n Charlie built still stands like a watchtower near the dirt lane at its junction with the now hard-surfaced road to town. Almost square and high as a two-story house with an attic, it fends off encroaching woods. Most of the tarpaper plastered on the barn's exterior to seal in heat has sloughed off, exposing the vertical, weathered boards set atop a concrete-and-cinderblock foundation. Sweet-gum and pine saplings sprout from beneath the foundation; trumpet vines and Virginia creeper climb the grey boards with green vitality and curl over the tin roof. Four flues, one at each corner, jut upward from the roof; two wear their original caps of flatly conical, pierced metal. The barn door, cut so low that anyone entering to check the boxy, kerosene-fired furnace would have had to stoop, is padlocked.

Not long ago—no time at all on the river's clock—the barn was a humanly busy place. Joe Hill, a black man who helped work the farm from Miss Carrie's youth to her old age, remembers the sweat and friendliness of hard labor. I ask him how old he is. He purses his lips. "I ain't gonna tell you." So, I tell him my age, and he relents. "I'm younger'n you. Be eighty-seven this August."

Joe Hill, almost always referred to by both names, lives in a green-trimmed white trailer inland from the Point. It's set in an overgrown, treeless field where corn and tobacco used to be cultivated. Unfiltered sunlight floods the living room where Joe Hill leans back on a beige sofa, his hands on a cane. Overhead a ceiling fan rotates slowly, stirring the hot, thick air. His whiskery face is lean and young-looking; his age is attested by the thinning, grizzled hair atop his burnished brown pate. As if he wants to make doubly sure that his immaculate gabardine pants won't fall down if he decides to rise, he wears not only a wide leather belt around his considerable girth but suspenders over his short-sleeved red plaid shirt. The belt is unbuckled.

"Yeah," he says softly and nods his head. The word runs like a slow refrain through his telling. It's the same assent that punctuates the preacher's sermons in a black church. "When I started puttin' 'bacca down there, we tied it on a horse or used a mule pullin' a sleigh. They got 'bacca trucks these days. We sticked the 'bacca up and hung it in the barn and cured it. Yeah. Lot of hard work in it 'cause we had to get up in the mornin' 'bout four o'clock, three-thirty, take that 'bacca to the barn, put it on the rafters. My wife Lucy got up, got the hams, and cook breakfast. Well, Lord have mercy, if you'd tell somebody to do that now, they'd cuss you out. And all these white folks 'round here, that's how they got their livin's, just like that. Yeah, that's the way we lived."

Before the tobacco leaves were picked and loaded on the mule-drawn sleigh, a mortal lot of effort went into making the crop. Joe Hill drove horses or mules through the fields to plow and till the soil, and he set out the plants. His children and Miss Carrie's—and later, the grandkids—were sent to the fields to chop back weeds and pull the suckers and the fat green worms from the plants by hand. When the tobacco grew thigh-high, its broad leaves spaced in ascending layers on the stout stalks, the same armies trooped through to top these plants by hand-severing the flowers that pop up like huge white dandelion puffs above the leaves. Topping tobacco is still accomplished by hand, but chemicals eliminate the suckers and the worms that took so many sun-baked, aching hours to pluck off. After topping came lugging—picking the sand-lugs, the dirtiest leaves, in the layer closest to the gritty soil. Adults never did the lugging; it was kids' work because they were built closer to the ground. Then the plants were cropped—picked—with leaves from the upper layers of each plant taken two or three at a time as they ripened. After being loaded on that sleigh—or slide, as some call it, the leaves were pulled to the barn for flue-curing.

When tobacco was delivered to the barn, other people took over. The hander gathered four or five leaves at a time and gave them to the stringer who tied them with twine on a tobacco stick, a square pole four or five feet long. When the stick was full, a mover would take it to the barn where hangers put it across the rafters with the other sticks in tiers starting just under the barn's roof. When the barn was full to bursting, the furnace—wood in the Point's earlier days, kerosene later—would be fired, and the hands would move on to the next barn. Someone stayed to tend the furnace day and night till the leaves were dried. The curing job is done these days not in family barns but in larger, commercial facilities.

Miss Carrie's slim, bright-blonde granddaughter Rita Fay says, "The only crop I had to work on this farm was tobacco—tyin' tobacco on those sticks from six-thirty in the morning till they let you stop. I used to crawl up on the rafters in the barn, I was so tired. Fall asleep up there and *no*body could find me."

Her older sister, plump, blonde, and good-hearted Gwen, says, "I didn't mind tobacco, except for pullin' off the worms. It was choppin' cotton that I hated, hoeing out all those goddamn weeds. When the tobacco was curing, all us kids would go into the barn and get those little golden leaves that fell off. We'd roll 'em and smoke 'em."

"And there came Mama," says Rita Fay. "She did the beating. She'd tear you up."

Gwen nods and lights a cigarette. "She'd whip your heinie if she caught you smokin'." Mama had the implement for administering a proper smack, a handmade wooden paddle with holes drilled in it. Gwen indicates with her hands that it was as big around as a tennis racquet.

The barn was good for more than drying out the leaves to a crisp gold, more than giving a tired child a place to snooze atop a rafter. Joe Hill says, "We raised tomatoes and picked 'em and put 'em in quart jars. Set 'em in the 'bacca barn and sat 'em on the furnace. They cook. Whenever I kept my 'bacca route, I go there and screw the top down on 'em good. We got canned tomatoes. Yeah."

Miss Carrie and Cap'n Charlie's acres of immensely fertile, sandy loam produced money crops other than tobacco. Joe Hill ticks off a list. "Cotton, corn, sweet potatoes, soybeans—that's what we raised for a livin'. For ourself, we raised our hogs and our milk cow and chickens. We could catch all the fish you want to eat, and oysters. If we wanted some beef, we'd go kill us a deer, yeah. Raised our May peas and string beans. My own wife Lucy, my splendid wife, she put up a lot of stuff, fruit and everything."

I see the fruit, can almost taste it: peaches and large, grainy-textured pears still bend the boughs of fruit trees at the Point. A brown thrasher nested this year amid the greenbriar and honeysuckle vines enwrapping an ancient but still-bearing pear tree that stands beside the trailer where Miss Carrie's son-in-law Henry spent his later years.

Joe Hill bent himself to farming amid a legion of other laborers, grown and small. Those who didn't own land were sharecroppers, working someone else's farm not for wages but a portion of the harvest. He talks about those days: "Miss

Carrie's grandkids, they daddy Henry and they mother and my young 'uns, we puttin' our backs together. Henry helped me and I helped him. Eleven children I had, nine livin' and two dead. And forty-nine grandkids when my Lucy died— been more since then. And Henry had thirteen kids. If somethin' got ripe in my garden worth havin', he'd go down there and get it. People ain't friendly like that now, no sirree."

"Miss Carrie hated my mother, *hated* her, because she married Henry," says one of Henry's thirteen children.

But, oh what a handsome man! Small and slender, he looked at the world with rakehell nonchalance and a come-hither glint.

"Blue eyes, he had, but not pale blue—sky blue," says Rita Fay. Her own eyes are bright blue.

"Huckleberry eyes," says blue-eyed Gwen. "Deep huckleberry blue."

"He had magnetism," says a neighbor who knew him. "He was charming even when he was falling down drunk."

A photograph, late '40s or early '50s, on the mantel of his daughter Eva's double-wide shows Henry in Sunday-go-to-meeting garb. He stands jauntily, favoring his bad right leg. His three-piece suit with baggy, wide-cut trousers is old, but the sparkle on his lean and handsome face is as bright as a new-minted silver dollar. No wonder Miss Carrie's only surviving daughter Lena disobeyed her mother's often repeated wish and went ahead and married him anyway. In the photograph, Lena stands dark and matronly on Henry's left. His smile, his trim and unweathered good looks say he's discovered what Ponce de Leon could not, but Lena has been pushed prematurely into stout, purse-lipped age by childbearing, child-rearing, and baking batches of seventy-four biscuits twice a day from scratch. A second photograph, propped centrally on the mantel beside this one, shows an earlier Lena with her grandmother Mary Grover. In the 1920s, the teenaged Lena bloomed lush as a floribunda rose. A healthy, pretty, black-haired girl clad in skirt, striped overblouse, and patent pumps, she smiles and hugs a fox terrier in the crook of her right arm. On her left stands her tiny grandmother, whose white, skinned-back hair emphasizes the bones of a small, worn face, whose hand-sewn and starched ankle-length dress recalls the turn of the century. Lena herself was born in 1907. In the 1950s photo, she is in her early, weary forties. At the age of fifty-one, a heart attack will kill her. These two photos are the only ones on Eva's mantel that recall old times. They are surrounded by likenesses of later genera-tions, Eva's children and grandchildren, the great- and great-great-grands of Miss Carrie. Any photo of her is conspic-uously missing.

When Lena and Henry wed—she was eighteen, he twenty—against Miss Carrie's wishes, they stayed right here under Miss Carrie's disapproving eye. They lived in a succes-sion of tenant houses, Henry sharecropping for Cap'n Charlie and others, Lena helping and baking those biscuits and bear-ing child after child—thirteen, one of whom died in infancy, in a short twenty years. The first child, Clara, named for Henry's mother, was born on Lena's twentieth birthday.

Of that baker's dozen of children, four maintain homes at the Point, one visits and lingers as often as she can, four live elsewhere in reasonable urban prosperity, and four lie in the earth. The grave of Ernest Ray, 1928-1979, eldest son and sec-ond eldest child, is situated facing the river in the side yard of Joe, the thirteenth child, Lena's favorite, the one she called her "eyeball." In summer, gladiolas bloom orange beside Er-nest Ray's grey granite tombstone, and a pink tea rose blushes before it. The epitaph reads:

BE NOT SAD THAT I AM GONE,
I FOUGHT A HARD BATTLE
THE PRICE OF PEACE IS MINE.

The price he paid was cancer. He has gone to a reward more ethereal than the one he grubbed for in his healthier

84

years, the treasure promised on this very spot by the money light.

Ernest Ray's grave came first, then Joe's house, however odd and eerie it may seem to dwell beside a brother's place of escapades and later burial. But the grave is only the latest, and last, in a community cemetery used from the latter part of the nineteenth century until at least the mid-1920s. With the exception of Ernest Ray's gleaming stone, the markers have disappeared. The last two, both of lichen-mottled limestone, vanished mere months ago, perhaps to make Joe's yard look less funereal. With an inscription from the Beatitudes, one of the two stones commemorated a James Jackson, 1842–1895; the other, without epitaph, a Sallie Boswell, Feb 7, 1843–May 14, 1923.

Joe's wife Lana has inquired about these two graves. No-nonsense Lana, born in West Virginia as the daughter of a miner who was moved from coal-town to coal-town at his company's command, founded a drywall-contracting business with Joe, and she wields considerable executive power over this enterprise that supplies the Point's current residents with the five-gallon pails that once held joint compound and now hold everything else—fish, crabs, tomatoes, fresh water when a power failure threatens. Drywalling is manifestly successful, for it supports quite a few of Joe and Lana's kinfolk. These days Lana's hands wear elegant, diamond-clustered cocktail rings, sometimes two to a finger, and she drives a Mercedes. She can shoot a rattlesnake between the eyes.

"Jackson," she says, "that's a local name. The Jackson family—he may have been one of them—owned and sold the land where the Cherry Point Marine base stands now. But Boswell, it's not from around here. I had to ask and ask before I found anyone who'd heard of her. This is just a story, mind you, but I was told that she was a black woman born in slavery times, and somewhere in her younger days she was blinded in an accident. Later, she lived the other side of Courts Creek in a log cabin. The teen-aged boys around, they used to help her tidy up her place, sweeping, spreading clean sand on the floor. In exchange, she gave them—well, let me call it sex education."

So, in this part of the segregated south, just as black and white had put their backs together for work in the fields, they lay side by side in death. And probably in life as well; the neighbors, oldtimers and newcomers alike, say, "Everybody who grew up in these parts is related, I mean *every*body." It was in the community cemetery, over the colorblind graves, that the money light shimmered and danced and tantalized Ernest Ray, his younger brother Billy, and Joe Hill. Variously, the neighbors tell about the money light.

"Unexplained lights—foxfire, phosphorescence," says Mo. "But people believed it showed above a place where money was buried. You didn't follow it, though, when you saw it shining because, if you did, it'd kill you."

"The jack-o'-m'lantern, I've heard about that all my life," says our neighbor Tom's fishing companion Burt, whose life began seventy-one years ago on an inland farm. "My grand-daddy—he was on the water most of his life—said a boat all lit up would come out of the water toward shore and then disappear. I've seen that myself, but wouldn't none of the boys go down there with me. Granddaddy also saw a light on our land and found a stump all burned down. In it there was a bunch of silver money."

Eva's husband, a seagoing man who captained a dredge up and down the east coast and in such exotic waters as the Orinoco, says this: "I'll tell you the truth. Where there's a light, money's buried. Blackbeard the pirate, he knowed every shoal in Pamptico Sound. He buried money around here, and jewelry, and they claim a light will burn to it. And the house my father had—a hill by it and a graveyard. Some of my brothers and sisters saw the light there, looked like a fire burnin'. I never saw it, but they gone down there the next day and found no ashes or nothing like that."

Mo takes a puff on his pipe. "Marsh gas. Superstition."

But Gwen insists that her brothers and Joe Hill went digging in that cemetery till they found not one but two jars full of old coins. "They dug there, they dug everywhere—graveyards, back in the woods by the hermit's house, down by the creek. But they hid the jars, and nobody's seen them since."

Mo's daughter Bonnie swears she's seen the money light on dark nights, not at the Point itself but shimmering six or eight feet in the air on the curve by the last road before you turn off and come down to the river. Others say you can see it now, 'way back over the woods where the hermit lived out his last years.

The hermit, Herbert Briggs—no one knows why he took to a loner's life, but he was a fixture in the area for decades. He'd long kept to himself in a house he'd rented, a tenant house built to face in proper fashion the farm-to-market road. But one day, returning from an errand, he found that his eviction notice had been served—his worldly goods had been thrown on the side of the road. At that, Herbert Briggs removed himself into the deep woods, carved out a tidy clearing, and built a shed, in which he lived flank to haunch to udder with his mule and his milk cow. Yearly he made sure of his milk supply by taking his cow to a bull; he'd station her beside the fence enclosing the bull's pasture and wait till the bull sniffed the air and eagerly broke down the fence. For a hermit, he was right sociable, riding his mule out of the woods to accept frequent supper invitations from Miss Carrie and Cap'n Charlie. It's said, though, that when he entered the house, it was like to have tilted when all the occupants hurried to the far side of the room because Herbert Briggs washed neither the clothes he wore nor the clothes he was born in. Maybe the aroma helped when he got snake-bit out there in the woods: he always healed, but the snakes died. For all his touch-me-not ways, he was a kind-hearted man, bringing sacks of groceries to Miss Carrie and her grieving family whenever there was a funeral within the clan. Timber-company pines grow on his clearing now.

*   *   *

The hermit's woods, graveyards, and a teasing light—I suspect that Mo is right when he mentions marsh gas, but I'm enchanted by the game—the glimmering after the will-o'-the-wisp, the chasing after moonshine. Ernest Ray and crew may not have found the money but they did find the moonshine. In fact, they made it.

To this day, Harlowe, at the junction of Highway 101 and the twelve-mile road to the Point, is known as the place where you can get yourself a jug of 'shine—that is, if the dealer knows you. You're supposed to be able to tell where it's for sale by counting the pillars on the front porch of a house; the pillars are constructed so that one may be easily removed: four in place, stay away, but three—we're open for business. When I do occasional shopping in the big city of New Bern, the clerk at Montgomery Ward or the manager of Penney's, summoned to approve my check, will ask what area is represented by mail route number one out of Havelock. I know that saying Adams Creek or Great Neck Point will draw a blank, so I tell them, "Harlowe." The sure response is, "Harlowe! That's where they make moonshine." When I ask lightly if they've put in a personal supply lately, they answer unanimously, "No way. I value my life." Our neighbor Tom says that as far afield as Boston, Massachusetts, he's had whispered offers of moonshine—"the best there is, made in Harlowe, North Carolina."

The tales of bicycle-riding lookouts on the twelve-mile road to the river may well be true, but local talk has it that stills are not so common as they used to be. The light, single-engine aircraft that flies low overhead at night without turning on its marker lights is manned by the sheriff's department, and it uses infrared to spy out a newer source of fast money—the marijuana plantations that certainly decorate the woods and clearings with potent, revenue-producing leaves and blossoms on stalks as big as tree ferns. Such searches are also conducted by National Guard helicopters and aircraft op-

88

erated by the State Bureau of Investigation. Whoever uses it, the equipment used to detect illegal gardens can also home in on the heat generated by fermenting mash and the fires burning under the still.

At the Point, 'shine was manufactured at least as recently as ten years ago, when Ernest Ray and Billy ran a still in broad daylight behind the trailer in which Gwen lives now. As for today, Jim the waterman swears that the sour scent of mash blew from the woods on a southeast wind when he fished the Rounding last summer. And the Point's resident part-time deputy says, "There's a little bit of 'shine tucked in the woods right now. I wouldn't have to walk a hundred yards 'fore I could find you some. I wouldn't get near that liquor, it'd rot your gut."

Manufacture, like fieldwork and burial, was an integrated enterprise giving no clawhold to Jim Crow except in the matter of who went to jail. At the mention of secretly concocted firewater, the clan's memory springs instantly to a tale of Cap'n Charlie, his younger son Sheldon, Joe Hill, and Gilbert, who was married to the sister of Joe Hill's wife. "Granddaddy and our uncle and Joe Hill always made liquor—moonshine liquor. One time they were running off a batch over in the backwoods near the creek, and Gilbert, he was supposed to be the lookout. Well, the revenue officer came. Gilbert saw him all right, but he got so wrought up, he stuttered—he stuttered anyway—and he couldn't, he could *not*, tell 'em that the law was there. Joe Hill felt that something was going on, though. So he swam on the other side of Courts Creek, but they got him. They got him six months in jail."

In her soft, sweet voice, Gwen tells how once upon a time she and her siblings gave innocent assistance in the long-distance transport of moonshine from the Point. "Some of us kids went with Daddy to Virginia on the back of a truck. It was loaded with cabbages, and we sat on top. How could we know that it was liquor underneath?" Heads of cabbage and towheaded children, what camouflage for a load of gullet-searing, brain-addling, pure white lightning! But each jug of contraband may have been seasoned with a peach to take off the bite and give a sweet corn liquor.

"Or you could put an apple in it," says Rita Fay. Tom's fishing friend Burt has another preference. "Hard rock candy—makes that corn so go-o-o-d you cain't resist."

The biggest 'shine operation about which anyone is minded to speak openly occurred at the end of the '60s. Like pursuit of the money light, it promised a cure for poverty. "I remember times we were so goddamn hungry we could have eaten *this!*" Rita Fay's hand grabs a wooden porch rail; her knuckles are white. "Granny gave us nothing. My father lay up there with half a leg and maggots crawling in it, but did she give us shit? Granddaddy used to steal some lard, corn meal, anything to feed us." Her eyes narrow and her jaw tightens. "My children will *never* be poor."

In 1968—a year after Cap'n Charlie had died, three years after Sheldon had climbed into his truck, driven off to the VA hospital in Winston-Salem, and come home shortly thereafter in a coffin—one of the thirteen, a married brother prospering in Virginia assumed somehow that he stood to inherit the farm. "Just by listening to Granny after Granddaddy had passed away," says another of the thirteen. "So he sunk a lot of money. He had his own business, and he'd saved a lot. What he did was buy a big John Deere tractor and hire on Joe Hill to work for him planting soybeans and tobacco and all that good stuff. But my brother wanted to make back the money he'd laid out for farming. Fast money. He went and bought all this equipment, everything imaginable, and he backed Joe Hill to set it up. My brother would come down once a week to see that Joe Hill had all the meal he needed and that the liquor was running off. My brother was gonna take it to Virginia, but all of a sudden it just blew up in their face. One of the neighbors—Mr. Sneaky Pete—got wind of it and snuck around till he found out what was going on and turned 'em in. The revenuers came down here, and they caught Joe Hill right at the liquor still running it off into half-gallon jugs. It was on TV. My brother, he paid his fine. Joe had to go to jail for it. I don't know what happened after Joe got out, if my brother gave him a certain amount of money or what. But my brother lost his ass here. He got so far in debt he had to file bankruptcy."

Joe Hill retired then from sweating on other men's farms; for the next twenty years, into his mid-eighties, he worked at a campground. But did the brother ever get the land? Yes, a small portion. At the time of Miss Carrie's death, the farmland she still held was divided among fourteen of her grandchildren.

But in 1968, at the time of the big-scale moonshine operation, Miss Carrie was ten years from her death. Nor did she have it her power to distribute to clamoring kin all of the acreage she'd inherited from her father. The river had claimed some cornfields and pushed the shoreline farther east. Then, sometime in the '40s, Miss Carrie had deeded much, if not all, of the farm's river frontage to her younger son Sheldon. He and his wife sold off a chunk of eight-plus acres in 1948. That chunk is the piece of land that stretches between our boundary line and Courts Creek; it's the land that held the house in which Miss Carrie played as a child, in which Henry and Lena lived when their daughter Eva was born in 1931. The hurricane of '33 demolished the house; since then, the land on which it stood has passed from family to foreigners and, finally, to the Nay-Sayer who presides in absentia over its ruination. Sheldon sold off other pieces of waterfront after that, a little at a time.

When Sheldon died, he was divorced and childless. The river-washed land that he hadn't sold reverted to Miss Carrie. She, too, starting no later than the mid-'60s, had cashed in on a lot here, another there. One of these pieces, conveyed by her to an outlander in 1966, is the acre that now puts me and the Chief on river time.

*   *   *

Of the Point's farming days, little is left to remind the newest
frontier that they ever existed. There's the tobacco barn, of
course, a support now for vines and a shelter for feral cats.
And behind Ed and Beulah's cottage, there's a board-and-bat-
ten smoke house where hams were cured in the heavy fumes
of long-burning, green oak logs laid atop pitch logs of pine,
which kept the fire alive. An old rule-of-thumb stipulates that
the oak trees used for smoking hams be cut down when the
leaves turn scarlet in the fall, not coincidentally the time at
which hogs have always been slaughtered. The smoke house,
according to Ed's reasonable guess, was put up just after the
turn of the century. By its door he has nailed the rectangular,
black-and-yellow sign that designates a fallout shelter. "Because," Beulah says, "that's where all the junk he accumu-
lates falls out."

The third relic is Mo's barn. The smaller section of the
ground floor, covered by a sloping extension of the peaked
roof over the loft, was once the pack house. There, hands
sorted the cured tobacco, bundled it by tying a soft, undried
tobacco leaf around each handful of stems, and wrapped the
bundles in burlap for transport to a warehouse. The same,
slant-ceilinged space must also have sheltered implements—
plough and harrow, wagon and mule-drawn sleigh. Draught
animals were stabled in the larger section, where fodder and
harnesses were likely kept as well. (The milk cow had her
own shed elsewhere.) Over the stall stretched the hayloft,
where moonshine is said to have been stored, where a local
family later found refuge for the week it took the water
to recede after the hurricane of '70. Mo and his tribe use the
loft now as an attic for stashing things not good enough to
keep around the house but much too good to throw away.
The one-time pack house acts now as a shop for Mo's small-
engine-repair business; chain saws, lawn mowers, and garden
tractors, many of them venerable models, wait patiently inside and outside for his attention. The stalls in which horse

and mule and possibly an ox swished their tails are now filled with salvaged lumber; one holds a child-sized bicycle. The walls are decorated with the eclectic enthusiasm of someone who cannot bear to cast off any potentially useful object: crosscut saws, a kerosene lantern, a heating coil for an electric stove, shovels, gill nets and stray cork floats, two foot-and-a-half long anchors of the type called eelhead. Dinette chairs and bushel baskets, a stack of shutters and a western saddle and you-name-it clog the aisle between the stalls. Mo used to keep a few animals here, a mixed herd of milk goats and Red, the gelding that his youngest daughter rode when early adolescence inflamed her with the wish to be a Centaur. Dust sits in the saddle these days, and the horse is long gone. The last goat, a mostly black Toggenburg nanny with hips jutting skyward like mountain peaks, died two years ago. Sal Doberman sniffs at their phantom scents.

"Don't know when the barn was built," Mo says as he putters with an out-of-whack carburetor, "but the first time I ever came down here—in '54 when I was discharged from the Marines after Korea—the house we live in was under construction. But the barn was old then, old." Ed thinks it's contemporary to the smoke house, turn-of-the-century vintage.

Miss Carrie's house, her last home on the Point when it was still a farm, is the fourth and least aged reminder of the old days. She and Cap'n Charlie lived there from the time of its completion in the '50s till she sold it, along with the barn and some piney woods, to Mo and Joyce in 1967. Standing on the third tier back from the river, it is shaded by generous hackberry tree, a warty bark as they call it here. The hermit dug it as a sapling in the woods and brought it here by oxcart as a housewarming gift to Miss Carrie. When Mo and Joyce first saw the house, the siding was painted a cool, pale green. On its porch, Cap'n Charlie had sat and rocked and nodded laconically at passersby till he became so sick that he took to his bed. He died several years after that in the downstairs master bedroom, in which Joyce and Mo now sleep. The siding is repainted a green just lighter than forest green, a green the color of hackberry leaves. The old porch is gone, but Mo has constructed a new one, with screens and storm windows. Cap'n Charlie, however, may still be there; Mo's daughters think he is. When each of them turned eighteen, Joyce commissioned a formal portrait. These paintings hang on the living room wall, always—almost always—perfectly aligned, for Joyce is a tidy housekeeper. But when a daughter has committed an error—received a traffic ticket or tried to pull a fast one, her portrait goes askew. Now who could be doing the tilting if not Cap'n Charlie?

Joyce tells about the day, that gol*lee* hot day in August, that she and Mo first saw the house and met Miss Carrie. "We came out to visit friends who had a place down here. We were really impressed by the Shangri-la feeling—so quiet, so desolate, so out of the way, and we asked our friend Peggy if there was any place for sale. 'Funny you should ask,' she said— she'd just brought Miss Carrie back from a visit to Raleigh. The house had been broken into, it was too lonesome in the country, and Miss Carrie wanted to sell.

"So Peggy introduced us, and we went in. There was Miss Carrie in her clean housedress and her hose. She talked to me and Mo—she was so sweet and precise, full of 'honeys' and 'sweeties.' We found out later that she dipped snuff and spit it in a little can she carried with her, but you wouldn't know it, you never saw the juice running out of her mouth.

"Anyhow, that hot hot day, there was a terrible smell in the house. We could not understand it. The house was sparsely furnished but spotless, with the shiniest oilcloth on the kitchen table. Miss Carrie was mortified. Then we found the beer cans in the washing machine. The people who'd broken in went and had themselves a party, too. Mo and I took the cans and emptied them at the dump on the way back to town."

They made an offer for the house and land. It was accepted; they moved in the following February. And they dug a well, installed a septic system, and put a house trailer in the back yard. Miss Carrie lived there for the next two or three years till she decided to move to Oriental across the river to stay with her sister Sadie.

The neighborhood voices rise like a Greek chorus to praise or damn Miss Carrie in her later years.

"I knew her real well, used to eat with her and take her shopping. She was a little tiny lady—slim."

"Petite and grey-headed, with a blue rinse. Very neat. Always wore a starched apron in the house."

"Kids at school would ask us where we live. How could you tell them we lived out here in nowhere? So we said, 'Adams Creek.' Granny heard that, and she said, 'Don't you never say that. You're not from any creek, you're from the river. Don't you forget it—the river.'"

"Feisty, that's what she was."

"Married at thirteen—I heard that Cap'n Charlie would come home wanting his dinner but she was playing with dolls."

"Married so young, but she didn't talk like an uneducated person."

"She had her favorites, no time for anybody else. Sheldon, he was her eyeball."

"You know how people talk—it goes from the pecan tree to the ditch bank. Everybody says she had a sweetheart in her later years. She sold him the piece of land right next to the barn."

"Sweetheart! That man was her lover, if you want the truth."

"I don't know about the romantic involvement, but he was a great comfort to her."

"To those of us who moved here, she was like our mother. She taught me how to fry corncakes. She'd mix up corn meal and drop it in hot oil while I fried us some fish."

"Miss Carrie used to go down through my yard, go

fishin' with a flounder light. Lots of flounder in them days, yeah."

"Used to see Miss Carrie and her sweetheart out there on the river evenings sitting in a boat and fishing."

The talk goes indeed from the pecan tree—pronounced PEA-can, not pe-CAHN—to the ditch bank and back again. All of it contains subjective truth, plumped up or tainted, according to the speaker. To me, the fundamental truth seems this: that Miss Carrie presided, however unwittingly, over the end of one era and the beginning of the next. She was the very gateway between the old and the new. When she played as a child in the farmhouse blown away much later in the hurricane of '33, the boats were freighting money crops and towing the log-rafts upriver to New Bern. Livelihoods at the Point depended on the mules and the hands in the fields and the men wielding saws to fell timber for boards and pulp-wood. They depended on self-sufficiency in almost every-thing, from raising hogs and forging necessary tools to mashing the corn to make strong drink. She saw the freight boats on the river dwindle and disappear, the braying mules replaced by snorting tractors, and the dust and mire of the road to town covered by prim asphalt. There must have come a slow moment, sometime after Lena and Henry had started rearing their prodigious brood, when she understood, per-haps in her heart rather than her head, that corn in its tas-seled rows was green as dollar bills but it didn't spend in the same way. Selling the land to foreigners could ease the cash crunch.

A neighbor who bought a half-acre on the river in 1965 says, "A drastic change came in, life took a real big turn when Sheldon died. At that point most of the waterfront was sold off. But that's when people really started moving in. Before he died, we used to come down here weekends and never see a soul."

With Sheldon, her eyeball, the last of her nine children gone, Miss Carrie sold the few lots remaining on the river and started accepting the offers tendered for the inland tiers. The fish-camps of the foreigners—the school buses, the shanties tacked onto trailers—had begun to clutter the shore in the '50s, though the back fields still nourished long, straight, green rows of corn and tobacco. Sawmills dismantled, and the logging camps where Sheldon had exercised his corded muscles, the woods were quiet, except when the big timber companies sent in mechanized crews to cut and run. With the sale of inland tiers, the nucleus of the present community arrived and stayed, the money in its pockets coming from work at Cherry Point, military retirement checks, and retail merchandising—hardware, groceries—in Havelock. The new frontier has comforts the old one never dreamed of—freezers, air-conditioners, satellite dishes. The foreigners, however, have not scared off the polecats and the hogbears.

"I asked Miss Carrie why she didn't keep any land on the river for herself," Mo says. "She told me she never put much stock in riverfront—she used to pick corn out there where the water is."

Kitchen gardens now grow luxuriant beside the trailers and permanent houses. The rich soil of the still considerable fields sprouts equally luxuriant weeds; rattlesnakes stalk mice there, and a male meadowlark installs his harem yearly amid the Johnson grass and thistles. The potential for commercial farming of these fields outlasted Miss Carrie by several years. The last tobacco crop was harvested the summer before she died; tobacco, however, could still have been planted till the early '80s, for the federal government had blessed the fields with the allotments that permit such planting. Miss Carrie's grandchildren inherited the allotments along with their shares of her land. But Rita Fay and Gwen's sister Emily put an end to the potential.

Bonnie tells me, "Emily was sick and near dying. Maybe she wanted some money for hospital bills or a last fling. Anyhow, she sold a strip running clear through the middle of the fields. And when that happened, the county rezoned the land from farm use to subdivision. The allotments were lost."

The Chief now grows our vegetables on the part of the strip that belongs to our neighbor Tom and runs from the back line of his riverfront place to the dirt lane. The section of strip on the other side of the lane, the section that divides the field almost dead center, belongs to Lena's eyeball Joe. And here, three years ago, Joe constructed the house on stilts. Joe's elder son lives there with his wife and their baby daughter—Miss Carrie's great-great-grandchild.

On the way back from town I pause seven miles from the river at Oak Grove Methodist Church. Its fresh, white country clapboards delicately reflect the green of grass and leaves. A slow-growing live oak, huge enough to have been a sapling as long ago as colonial days, shades the portion of the church-yard used for burying. Headstones crowd on initialed footstones, and most are set in a fashion I've not seen else-where. The side of the headstone that faces the footstone is blank; the inscription is carved on the side that looks away from the grave.

Henry lies there commemorated by no stone at all, but his grave commands attention as immediately as did the liv-ing, breathing, blue-eyed charmer who could cuss the stripes off a bullfrog. His tomb is almost imperial, a brick vault rising well above the ground, with the top of each end-wall stepped like a Mesopotamian ziggurat. This monument was built by Joe Hill's sons.

Such imposing vaults are popular not just in Oak Grove's cemetery but in burying grounds and house-yards throughout the area. "Above the ground," says Gwen, "let me tell you that's the only way they'll bury *me*." I ask her why—to be like her daddy? She pulls back at the foolishness of the question but relents and says, "I want to look my best."

Beneath a modest granite marker, Lena lies beside Henry and two of their six sons. A host of family clusters 'round, Claude and Sheldon, Cap'n Charlie's brothers, and Cap'n

Charlie himself, all memorialized by the neatly carved, grey silences of names and dates. One date holds another small truth: Cap'n Charlie was only five, not fourteen, years older than Miss Carrie; a ripe eighteen when he married her, he must always have seemed somehow old, a man of reserve and premature solemnity. The epitaphs on these stones, if any, are tight-lipped, mostly offering a conventional "Asleep in Jesus." Within hugging distance, several small, diamond-shaped stones set on tiny marble plinths mark special graves: in the Oak Grove churchyard, this design remembers the babies. Two such diamonds snuggle close to Cap'n Charlie, closer still to Miss Carrie. Resting under earth, she is as much the graveyard's matriarch as she was the Point's: five of her nine children, several of her grandchildren, surround her still center. Polished granite roses glisten above her name; below her dates of birth and death, 1888–1977, the epitaph states in bold capitals:

SHE HATH DONE WHAT SHE COULD

Yes, she did. The statement holds an unintended irony but, yes, she did. And the effects still add a bitterness or sweetness to life on the Point. I like to imagine the grey-haired lady, sweet and precise, heading toward the river with flounder light in hand or sitting out there on the water with her grey-haired sweetheart. Perhaps they talked, perhaps they merely listened to the splash of fish or cast a line not necessarily to catch anything but just for the peacefulness of it. She was after all a woman from the river, not the creek. I think of her on the water stealing brief respite from the everlasting responsibilities and hard work and the clamor of needful or greedy voices. When the land became too much to bear, the river could always give surcease. It still does.

5
The River Provides

"THE GODS DO NOT deduct from the allotted time of man those hours spent in fishing." So goes the saying. If it holds a jot of truth, many people at the Point are doing their utmost to achieve immortality.

Summer dawn and summer dusk, the ends of the piers sprout fishermen, the young ones standing, their elders parked in folding lawn chairs, and all with bamboo poles or high-tech rods in hand. Nearly everyone has a couple of buckets nearby, those ubiquitous five-gallon buckets that once contained joint compound. Now their depths wait for fish or hold bait—cut-bait, shrimp, minnows seined or cast-netted at the creek, some of the red wiggler worms that Mo raises in his back yard. The feline population of the Point inevitably zeroes in on this bounty; fishing can become a matter of shooing off cats.

Pinfish most often hook themselves. They're thrown back or cut into bait. Small croaker are hauled in, and undersized puppy drum. Just as bluefish are named according to their size—snapper for the eight-inch babies, tailor for the pound-plus yearlings, puppy designates the frisky young red drum (also called channel bass or redfish, the latter appellation often preceded by the word "blackened"), a fish that can attain a weight of more than eighty pounds. Big drum are plugged out in the river, twenty pounds and up, but our inshore catch is the puppy. And when one at or just over the legal fourteen-inch limit is pulled in flapping its ocellated tail, the angler's whoops of surprised glee sound up and down the waterfront. Eels also strike hook-dangled bait and are usually discarded as soon as a hand succeeds in grasping the slippery, thrashing body so that the other hand can disgorge the hook. Their slime offends, and few river people consider them worth eating, though they are cut in chunks and put on hooks to lure more acceptable species. Summer flounder, the most prized fish hereabouts, take bait that's been put on the bottom. Most are throw-backs, no bigger than a child's palm, the kind we call fifty-dollar flounder because that's a nice round figure for the $47.50 fine assessed per fish if the wildlife officers find us with specimens under the legal thirteen inches. It's also possible to snag an old tennis shoe or a beer can.

Above all others, Ed advocates the use of rod and reel. Tagging along with his father to freshwater holes near Cairo, Illinois, he's fished since he was old enough to hold a pole. He's tried gill-netting but claims that all he can ever pull in is jellyfish and junk fish. So we look for him at the end of a pier or sitting in a lawn chair on the shore. He and Beulah are among the lucky few to have a handkerchief of sandy beach instead of a bulkhead. From this beach Ed practices what he calls with intentional fancy "surfcasting in the river." The river lacks surf in all but the wildest nor'easters, when no sensible person would be out fishing anyhow, but the technique is much the same: pull chair to water's edge, spin out a line, and wait. Shrimp is his bait, not artificial lures, and he catches all the croaker anyone could want. Nor is he often alone; like pelicans feather to feather atop pilings, he and his cronies perch elbow to elbow in lawn chairs on the beach. Taking a break from her housework, Beulah has glanced at this line-up and seen "all in a row, the backs of bald heads." Visiting, she says, is more the exercise's point than fishing. Ed states unequivocally that his favorite method of angling, bar none, is drift-fishing. For years, he's driven a series of low-powered outboard boats—"whatever we can afford, whatever will float"—beyond the shallows into deeper waters. He cuts the motor then, casts a line, and lets the river take him where it will. And where the croaker, spot, and blues begin to strike, there he drops anchor, reeling in fish, contentment, and a blue crab or two.

Ed's success with rod and reel eludes most of us. Hook-and-line fishing is not a reliable way to catch supper, though it is a key to relaxation, to letting the brain go into rhythms as slow and easy as the long swells that roll across the river's surface, as effortless as the rise and fall of the bottle-nosed porpoises that glide upriver on a quiet evening. To assure a catch, be it a few fish at a time or a massive, thousand-yard effort for the Harlowe VFD's twice-a-year fish fry, most of us set gill nets.

Slamming doors jar me out of sleep. The doors of pickup trucks, not cars, for the thunks are heavy, solid. Men's voices boom in greeting. My body's clock says that it's perhaps an hour after midnight. I won't rise, I will *not*, for I'm due to leave the river just after dawn to take a day-long examination for certification as an ambulance attendant. Oh my pesky curiosity, be calm! Rest is essential to success, and our isolated community needs on-the-spot medical services. But men keep talking, vehicles come and go, and I drift, sometimes submerged, sometimes bobbing on the surface of awareness, till daylight comes. The Chief's half of the bed has been empty all night.

Feet together, knees akimbo, he sits in the kitchen. His face, his whole body sag, and he's naked as a skinned eel. He groans when I say good morning. "Hon, what can you do for someone who's rubbed hisself raw?"

His inner thighs and genitals show an advanced case of diaper rash. I fetch the baby lotion. "Don't touch me," he says. "I'm too sore. I'll do it myself." As I breakfast, he tells me of the night's events.

"Drat Tom's hide. He went to bed and left his pier net out. Asked me to check it later because he could feel more fish striking as he pulled the first ones out. Blues, oh my gawd, blues."

Just after midnight, he'd taken a look at the net stretched from Tom's pier into the river. Marsh on marsh, the two hundred yards of tough nylon filament were clogged with bluefish, more than one person could possibly handle. Most were eighteen-inchers, on the large side for the river. He roused the neighborhood with pleas for help. Mo responded, to help him pull fish after fish from the mesh and clean them before they spoiled. Blues die quickly. In warm weather, decay comes almost on the heels of death; as soon as rigor passes, the soft, purply flesh begins to liquefy. In a matter of hours, bluefish reek.

He says, "Never saw so many blues at once. Stopped counting at two hundred and fifty. Mo took the big share, but, Hon, look in the freezer." The Chief shifts in the kitchen chair and grimaces. I know what's caused the chafing: extracting and cleaning fish from midnight till dawn in a wet jumpsuit.

Opening the freezer compartment in the trailer's refrigerator is like opening the legendary overloaded closet. A dozen packages of fillets tumble to the floor. Al pulls up in the yard and honks. Hastily, I crowd the fallen packages back into the freezer. The Chief rests weary head in hands. Al, Bonnie, and I depart for the exam.

To set a gill net is to put oneself on duty as long as the net stays in the river. In spring and autumn, the demands are not so urgent, for the water's chill affords cold storage for the fish, even those that die right after striking. Then, the fish can wait from ten PM till daybreak. But when mirage weather comes, river and land both shimmering with heat, the net set just before supper must be fished at dusk, midnight, perhaps at three AM, and certainly at dawn. Sometimes we fish right after supper: a splashing or corks pulled under announce striped mullet, puppy drum, or a nuisance fish like the long-nosed gar, close to a yard long, that sneak from pond and creek into the salty river. Some say that gar is edible; we've never put that statement to a test. Our neighbor Tom avoids the graveyard shift by setting his nets at dusk and boating them in three hours later to be fished ashore. Unless there's a large haul, he and his wife Merle have cleaned their catch by midnight and gone to bed. Others, we among them, stretch out nets and leave them in the water for as many as three days running. Everything else—sleepiness, headaches, rain, a rock-bottom case of the lazies—must be thrust aside. We set the net and put ourselves in thrall. No excuses; the net is a tyrant, for the fish won't wait.

Because the Chief is a nocturnal animal, while I turn into a pumpkin by eleven PM, our predilections easily divide our labors at the net: taking midnight duty, he sleeps when I wake to rejoice in sunrise. We occasionally borrow a boat more sturdy than our own light fibreglas johnboat to take our hundred-yard net into deeper waters where the blues and Spanish mackerel run far more abundantly than they do in-shore. More often, the Chief wades out the net while I stand onshore feeding him the corkline and attaching the net's near end to the bulkhead with a small Danforth anchor. The off-shore end is weighted with a concrete block. When time comes to pull the net ashore, we stand dryclad at the bulkhead and pull, the Chief gallantly hauling on the heavier leadline. On summer nights, the big brown bats zip overhead in our floodlight's bright beam, and the flapping bodies of netted fish glisten silver as they're pulled toward shore. When they're safely over the bulkhead, we extract them, putting edible species and baitfish into a cooler, tossing the others back home.

The River Provides

While the net is submersed off the bulkhead, we each fish at our chosen hours by wading out to its far end where the water is chest-high and working back. Mid-April to mid-October, the water is warm enough to feel like skin. A jumpsuit and long-sleeved shirt beneath it protect flesh from jellyfish stings, and old sneakers, algae-green from dampness, save feet from being cut by shells or broken glass. We both wear gloves—the Chief's are rubberized yellow nylon, mine white cotton string—because dorsal-fin spines can stab, break off, and stay in our hands like splinters and the sharp edges of gill coverings can slice like newly-whetted knives.

Clad in clothing and anticipation, I enter the early-morning river. On fair days, sunrise tints the water pink and blue. Other times, rain bounces off the water, repelled by surface tension, before it melts into the brine. And on some days, infrequent and cherished, fog closes in veiling the far shore. Without a horizon, water and sky merge into a single entity as pearly grey and gleaming as the lining of an oyster shell. I immerse myself in mystery, in a frightening beauty. Glass calm or roiling, the water scares me. Its surface blocks my gaze as air cannot. Who knows what swims therein or lies in predatory ambush? Stingray, toadfish that can crush oyster shells in its jaws, stargazer capable of administering electric shocks? All these and more we have seen, have handled, not always knowing at first what they were. And the opaque water spawns legends—a genie fished up in a copper jar, a flounder that grants wishes, Poseidon wielding the sceptre of his barbed trident to command the dolphins and the true mermaids.

Whatever the perils, whatever the weather, a red cooler, tied to my waist by a nylon line, tags along to hold the catch. At net's far end, I toe up the leadline, grasp it, and pull it upward so that the net lies flat on the water. Quick, slow, the speed of my movement toward shore depends as much on the distractions offered by the river as it does on the catch. Little pipefish, stick-straight relatives of the sea horse, drift along

105

the corkline, where shrimp also play, leaping over it, turning dizzy somersaults. Once I closed my hand around a brown shrimp resting on the corkline and put it in the cooler; it was long enough to fill a hotdog bun. Hardly so appetizing (though they are used as food in the Far East) are the jellyfish that cluster in sultry weather on the corkline thick as bees in a blooming persimmon tree. I watch the gap between my long sleeves and my gloves, for most are sea nettles, white or purplish, the tentacles of which pack the lash of a cat-o'-nine-tails, except that these cats don't stop at nine but can reach an extravagant forty. When the jellies swarm in, I must remind myself not to mutter at the catch as I'm wont to do, not to open my mouth at all as the net is fished, for lines and meshes pulled tight and then released can act as slingshots hurling fragments of stinging tentacles at the nearest targets, such as tongues and tender mucous membranes.

And as I work the net, the chatter of a kingfisher stitches an invisible line along the riverbank. A snowy egret chases minnows in the shallows near the sandbar at the creek mouth while a great blue heron joins the raucous train of gulls following a commercial crabber as he checks out his line. The porpoises roll by in a leisurely file, small ones at their parents' sides.

A gill net does exactly what its name implies: some fish that enter it stretch the mesh and, trying to escape by swimming in reverse, become trapped by their flaring gills. But that's not all. Others, like striped mullet, wedge their stout shapes in the filaments. Menhaden, which feed with mouths constantly agape to strain plankton from the water, "swallow" the net by closing their jaws upon it and not letting go. Still other fish, notably flounder and stingrays, thrash so vigourously that they basket themselves, wrapping the filaments around their bodies as if they'd cast themselves into string shopping bags. It can be fiendishly difficult, especially with barb-tailed rays, to unbasket them.

Fishing the net is like reading a novel of suspense. Eager

to know what happens next, I turn the net's pages. Speckled trout? Gizzard shad? A waterlogged board? Once we pulled out an eighteen-inch sturgeon, touched its rough, bone-plated hide, and let it go. These days the river's sturgeon are endangered. Till the last page is read, there's hope for a happy ending, a jack crevalle or a whopping five-pound puppy drum. Some days bring enough fish to keep me standing for hours at the cleaning table. Other days, I stand for hours in the water backing out inedible menhaden or wrestling with gar. Horseshoe crabs can spin cocoons of nylon netting around their lumbering, archaic bodies. I extricate them later, for they'll survive while the worthwhile catch is processed. Fish I can't identify go in the cooler. Tom is my encyclopedia. Silvery fish with body flat and narrow as a butterplate turned on its edge and eyes set high above the long, steep slope to its mouth? "You've got a lookdown." Small fish of brown-mottled beige that wears a tiny unicorn's spike in the middle of its forehead? "Filefish."

If we leave the tyrant net untended, we risk more than spoilage. The river teems with competitors. It's easy to tell if a fish has been preyed on by an eel or a turtle; turtles like to chomp off heads while eels, preferring something more visceral, go for the anal opening to clean out the body cavity. Blue crabs aren't so choosy; their vise-grip pincers mutilate fish wherever purchase is found. With dratted regularity, the crabs wrap themselves in the net's mesh; the secret of extracting them without injury to fingers and thumbs is to catch their claws and break them off before the claws catch us. The crab-couples known as doublers, large jimmies cradling little jennies, also use the net as a honeymoon resort. The jennies, called sooks in the up-north language of Chesapeake watermen, are about to molt into maturity. The salmon and purple colors striping their triangular aprons show that they'll soon burst from too-small shells and, in their new jelly-softness, they'll mate for the first and only time in their lives. In a gesture that seems like tenderness to human eyes but is really a practical device to ensure continuing blue-crabbiness, a jimmy keeps cradling a newly bred jenny, her apron now as round as the dome on a state house, till her shell hardens enough to armor her. Because the jennies bear the future of the species beneath their aprons, we shake them out but put the cradling jimmies and the lone males into the red cooler with the fish.

There is no end to competitors. Once in a while, always early in the morning, a grey-brown head pops out of the water and stares with dark, bright eyes. As it stares, it chews and its forepaws fiddle with something just under the surface: river otter, eating fish and ripping the net. Birds, too, come for the pickings. Gulls and pelicans paddle up to the corkline and go bobbing for fish as children bob for apples on Hallowe'en. The gulls are noisy as children, too, squealing and arguing. Osprey halt in the air, hover, and stoop on the trapped catch; sometimes, not often, they are also trapped. The bluefish come too. I've heard that only human beings and bluefish kill for sport, not food. A bluefish, crammed with meat but driven by irrepressible, instinctive appetite, keeps on killing, sinking needle-teeth into prey it does not want or need. We may not catch the bluefish, but we see the evidence of their attacks—a tail bitten off, a body chopped nearly in half.

On the way to the exam, I regale Bonnie and Al with my second-hand account of last night's stupendous catch. Bonnie lifts speculative eyebrows; she's thinking that Mo will make a properly paternal contribution to her larder. If he doesn't, he'll be importuned.

In the late afternoon, we return to the river slightly addled from hours of answering written questions and demonstrating to the examiners that we can indeed take blood pressures and pulses, check vital signs, affix splints, stanch bleeding, move a spine-injured patient, administer oxygen, and give CPR. The Chief has obviously cured his weariness with sleep, but he's walking oddly, his blue-jeaned thighs held wide apart.

108

Bonnie says, "You look like a man in dire need of our medical services."

The Chief admits to grievous disability caused by working in a wet jumpsuit.

"Galded!" Al exclaims. "That's what you are, galded!"

"You mean gelded," the Chief replies.

"Nope, *galded*. It usually happens in your shorts, but it can hit your armpits, too. I know just what you need." Al marches briskly to the overgrown back field and returns with a handful of ragweed. He gives it to the Chief. "Here, tuck this in your pockets. You'll feel better 'fore you know it."

The Chief makes a face but stuffs the ragweed in his side pockets. "I ain't sure I trust a man who pees on his own feet."

"Got rid of my athlete's foot, didn't it?" Al says cheerfully. "Just you wait."

Galded—I am intrigued by the word and the ragweed remedy. The few dictionaries that bother to list the word say it's obsolete, the past participle of *gall* with an extra -*ed* tacked on. It's a kissing cousin of *spaded*, the neutering done to female dogs, and *drownded*, as in a frog-drownding rain. Al picked it up in rural Indiana, and I've heard it before in Bull Pasture territory, a term probably imported from England in colonial days and now kept quite alive in nooks and crannies of the south and midwest. It fits in country mouths as comfortably as a wad of chewing tobacco. As for the ragweed, that cure may be as old as the affliction, but it's new to me.

The next day the Chief walks without waddling. In a week, he feels like a man again. The moral of the story is, Work dry, not wet. But the benefits are certainly worth the sore price paid: blues enough to keep us feasting winter-long.

After a season of hard use, a net becomes as ragged as a well-worn pair of blue jeans. The seams wedding net fabric to cork- and leadlines begin to part; the mesh is frayed and full of holes. The culprits are many: crabs wielding scissor-claws, snags popping the filaments, and human hands extracting

fish. And large creatures to whom thin nylon is merely a mo-
mentary impediment—sharks? rays? porpoises?—have
plunged right through, leaving four-foot rents in the mesh.
The fish slip through these gaps just as loose change slips
from a frazzled pocket. But unlike superannuated jeans, nets
can be repaired, new fabric for old. And we swing into a com-
munal event comparable to a corn-husking or a quilting bee.

Two yard-long wooden crossbars have been nailed to
pines twenty yards apart in our front yard. When the twine
securing tattered fabric to the sturdy lines of corded plastic
has been snipped and the old net discarded, the lines are
saved and suspended between the crossbars. Netting is sold
by the pound, and we've bought five-and-a-half pounds of a
heavy-gauge fabric that will last for a season, not just a month
or two. It's placed between the lines, and the net needles—
hand-held shuttles—are wound tight with fresh twine. We
begin then on a two-day, sun-up to sundown job. Expert net-
hangers could accomplish it with far more economy of time,
but the Chief and I are amateurs. We'll take all the help we
can get.

As it's wont to do on the river, help arrives. Barefooted
Merle, wearing her river costume of slacks and loose-fitting,
red blouse, picks up a net needle and makes for the corkline.
Tom's in his usual costume, too—jumpsuit and maroon cap to
keep the sun off his bald head. From the outset, he claims the
leadline. They live in New Bern but come to their place on the
river every Friday, heat or chill, after work. In no respect,
however, do they fit into Joyce's category of borrowing, beg-
ging week-enders who flee as soon as rain begins to fall. As
she has for twenty-some years, Merle comes to the river with
supper-invitations, homegrown vegetables to give away, and
items—"I thought you-all might like this"—that she's found
on sale. She's the source of our fillet-knives and the brown
plastic dishpan in which I thaw crabpot bait. And every Friday Tom, my encyclopedia, sets nets enough to supply everyone who helps him, and some who don't, with free fish. Tom

now maintains the beacons that guide aircraft into and out of Cherry Point; Merle keeps the books for a bank. On their days of rest from work, they donate their freedom to our work, this business of hanging a net.

What a tedious, repetitive, hypnotic business it is, picking up three loops of netting, measuring six inches—the length of our net needles—from the last knot, tying a clove hitch or a couple of half-hitches to the line, and picking up another three loops. To keep the netting straight, leadline and corkline are worked simultaneously, and the person handling the latter must remember to slide in a cork at the end of each finished yard. As each twenty yards are rehung, the completed section is pulled into a barrel, a capacious orange barrel donated by Tom's fishing friend Burt. Six inches at a time, a hundred-yard net becomes long as a country mile.

Or so it would seem, if not for the company and conversation. On a rotating basis, we have two to work, one to fetch cool drinks between rewinding empty needles, and one, recumbent in a lawn chaise, to supervise. Like any other activity on the river, this one draws its share of onlookers. We all talk.

Merle utters praises for the improvements technology has wrought in gill nets. Her grandmother was born and brought up in one of the maritime communities Down East. Anywhere else, that name would evoke Maine, but here it refers to the coastal area just south of the river where the barrier islands angle to the west and the people have been watermen for centuries. It used to be that hands, her grandmother's among them, were the machines that fabricated cotton string into fish-catching mesh and repaired the netting when it frayed or rotted, as it all too readily did. Hands twisted apart manila rope to insert lead weights; hands spliced the lines and fashioned corks. They whittled needles of varying lengths out of green hardwoods—one wood of choice was poplar—and let them dry to firm up before they were put into service. Now the needles are made of molded plastic, and the leadlines, made of plastic cord, come with weights already bound in.

Mechanical spiders spin out the lightweight nylon filaments. Nylon soaks up no moisture. How heavy those old cotton nets must have been, as laden with water as fish!

Tom's bronze-bearded namesake son drops by and lingers, the son who recycled the office-machine motor into his father's boat hoist. He hears the mention of Down East and perks up. The area preserves remnants of an antique way of pronouncing English, a colonial crispness not softened by any southern imprecision, a brogue that insistently converts every long *i* into *oi*. Mimicking the accent of Down Easters—he calls them Hoigh Toiders—Tommy lets fly with a few tales.

"One thing you got to understand about Hoigh Toiders is their background. They live on a deserted little sandpit down there. Only one road goes in, and it's three feet above sea level. So, they love hoigh toides. Every toime there's a storm, nobody can get to town and nobody can go down there, which makes 'em happy. They're only two generations removed from poiracy."

"First off, if you do get down there, the thing you notice about 'em is the way they talk. It takes a few days to understand the words they're sayin' 'cause some of 'em don't sound loike English. It's a sea-farin' community. Think about it—if you stand about a boat in a thirty-foive knot gale and it's thirty degrees outsoide and you're dipped half-frozen in salt water, troi to move *your* jaw. You'd talk just loike 'em."

As the descendant of a Down Easter, Tommy's entitled to satirize his kinfolk. Nobody hands him a net needle or bids him fetch a cold soda. His talk takes our minds off those slow six inches, loop and knot, loop and knot.

"Hoigh Toiders, they always tell the truth—except for this one fella Oi was talkin' to the other day. Told me that on the last nor'easter when the wind she was blowin' the salt out of you, the toide rose so hoigh out there on the south soide of the sandpit that he had to get his shad net out of the shed and set it 'tween the bean poles in his garden to keep the sharks out of his collards. Oi got a loikin' that this man moight loie to you."

Sharks—the river has shark stories of its own, though none includes the vegetarian that preys on collard greens. The only shark I've seen in these waters is the young sandbar specimen that tangled itself in Jake the Dog-Killer's net. After we'd inspected it, Jake tossed it back. Merle, still working along the corkline, reminds us of the bull shark, a three-hundred pounder, that was captured two years ago in the Intracoastal Waterway. "That's just around the corner, not three miles from here. I'd rather meet a collard shark." Bull sharks haunt the tidal shallows and freely swim up rivers, even into fresh water. They have been known to sink their teeth in human flesh, though no such attacks have been documented in the lower Neuse. Loop and knot, we debate the possibilities for meeting bull sharks in our bailiwick. The odds favor us, not leviathan, but we agree that it behooves us to be vigilant.

Other giants travel the river's broad road. Prime among them are mammals, the bottle-nosed porpoises (or dolphins—the words are basically interchangeable). These streamlined cynosures make almost daily parade in disciplined files, sometimes breaking ranks to feed or gambol—wild porpoises. Other herds that hug the ocean shore or cruise the nearby sounds are watched by marine researchers, who track their movements, feeding behavior, and reproductive habits. Members of these herds are captured so that their raked and triangular dorsal fins may be notched with individual patterns for later indentification. But no trained eye observes the river's porpoises, no hand has touched them; their fins are whole. Lured by tales of friendly sport between dophins and humankind, K.D. has swum out to make their acquaintance. They did not falter in their rolling stride.

Loop and knot, from his position on the corkline, Tom says, "Hope the dolphins don't ever get caught in that fella's nets. They'd drown." He's referring to the man in New Bern who sets wide-mesh gill nets made of nylon with a steel-like strength and catches tarpon. Last year a picture in the New Bern paper showed a 102-pound specimen he'd snared in his tough but nearly invisible web. None of the net-hanging crew has yet seen this speedy, agile, fighting game species in the river.

Our part-time deputy has wandered in. "Wouldn't want to see one," he says. "Tarpon, you don't eat them. Now red drum, that's something else. Used to have some big ones in the river, forty, sixty pounds, scales like silver dollars, and you had to scale 'em with a hoe."

I'm sure I'm hearing a whopper until Tom says, "That's right. Put 'em on the ground, set your foot on top, and wield that hoe. It's easier to skin 'em."

"We just don't have those big fish like we used to," the deputy says.

Tom concurs and says that over the last twenty years the fish have steadily diminished in quantity as well as size. "Used to be you'd put a net out, wait an hour, pull it in, and find fish in every other marsh. Now you're lucky if you find one every yard."

The net-hanging crew and the onlookers blame commerce for the loss—trawlers coming in from nearby ports, ports a hundred miles away, ports out-of-state, all pulling nets that sweep the river clean. Our catches do seem to dwindle to little or nothing for two or three days after a large invasion of trawlers. But overall? Do the Point's readings of general conditions well from intuitive accuracy or spring fully armed from nostalgia's always gleaming but imperfect brow? I've asked Fisheries specifically for confirmation or dismissal of the local perception that the river's fish have become fewer and smaller in the past two decades. I'm told that the river's salinity has been much affected in recent years by the widespread digging of drainage ditches; peaty coastal soils can act as giant sponges able to soak up a three-inch downpour and release it slowly, but with trenches, the river knows feast or famine, receiving sudden floods of fresh water or none at all. Only the most adaptable species of fish can contend with such fluctuations. And Fisheries suggests that I come to the office and check its annual reports of commercial catches. "We compile them," the man at Fisheries says, "by tallying what the fleets tell us. But you know fishermen—they lie."

Loop and knot, it's close to dusk. The gnats are out biting ankles; mosquitoes whine and zero in on every other unclad body part. Merle hands me the needle for the corkline and runs to fetch the bug spray. Her son Tommy swats a mosquito sucking on his arm. "Now, skeeters," he says, "Hoigh Toiders use 'em to tell the toime of year. If they're little skeeters, just messin' with your ears and bitin' you on the arm, it's early spring. But if they're landin' on your shoulder and gettin' oye contact with you 'fore they go for the neck, then it's late summer. You got to understand they grow 'em big as parrots down there."

The last word on skeeters comes from a lawn chair where the Chief is busily rewinding needles. "You hear about the one that landed at Cherry Point? Mechanics put a jet engine in it before they realized what it was."

With that, we fold up for the day, sixty yards hung, forty to go. The net is finished the following afternoon and stretched out from our bulkhead that night. The haul is minuscule: one gar (released and told never to return), two croaker, and one speckled trout. The next day sees better fortune, a large catch that includes a four-pound puppy drum and a fish we rarely net, a summer flounder. At each of these fishings, the net has also presented us with blue crabs wound in the filaments along the leadline. They have been using their scissors. In new fabric, small rents have already appeared. Such damage is expected, though; this fabric is tough, will last one season and maybe two. The Chief states a seeming paradox: "The more holes a gill net gets, the fewer it has."

Summer flounder are by far the river's most appreciated fish, the species that activates salivary glands to full stream and ignites pure greedy lust in hearts and eyes. Seldom, however, do the Chief and I catch one of legal size in the three-and-a-quarter-inch stretch of our net. Fifty-dollar specimens of this bottom-hugging camouflage artist wedge themselves overabundantly in the meshes along the leadline. They're survivors; they may have been trapped all night, but they're still chockful of vitality. Bidding them return when they've grown up, we release them. When we do net one of legal size, hooked perhaps by only one blunt tooth, it's cause for exhilaration and craftiness. A 'possum could take lessons from a flounder at feigning death. The fish's body lies inert, almost rigid, nor does its overshot lower jaw move. But disentangle it, remove the one restraining filament from that snub-tooth, and all pretense is over. It fights when it's lifted into air, it fights again and harder while the fisherman holding its slipperiness with one hand strives with the other to open the red cooler's tight-fitting lid. I've learned to insert a finger firm and deep inside one gill and apply thumb just as firmly to the outside. The fight resumes when flounder is transferred from cooler to cleaning table at river's edge, and that fish can flip itself back into the water—damn!—with the speed of a shouted expletive. Here, too, that finger must be hooked in gill. Then removal of the scales, small and shiny as flecks of mica, may begin, and the first cuts made with a filleting knife. Two longitudinal, dark-skinned fillets from the eyed side, two white as cream from the blind side, and where the meat has been cut away, the carcass is as rosy and translucent as a stained-glass window. It goes home to the river, and the crabs, eels, and other scavengers flock 'round.

Nets may be hung especially for catching flounder with mesh of larger stretch, five or more inches. Tom sets a two-hundred yarder in the shallows off the Nay-Sayer's shore, while Jim takes his farther upriver toward the Rounding. And they do trap a share of flounder, two here, four there, as well as a few blues, the occasional whopping puppy drum, and all too many of those pesky, net-swallowing menhaden, most of them too small to use even as crab-bait. But a flounder net's most abundant catch is the one least desired, cow-nosed rays. Except in the untended killer-nets, the rays are always alive, always intricately basketed, always to be treated with the utmost chariness so that their barbs may have no contact with vulnerable flesh. Aside from nets or angling with a hook and line, there are two other ways to bring in flounder, one intended and often rewarding, one always productive but as unpredictable as the advent of the leaning wind that shoves the water far offshore. Unlike that southeast wind, however, it happens more often than once every five years, and it's caused, one might say, by a lack of wind.

The first way is Miss Carrie's, traipsing into the night-time river with a gig and a flounder light. Summer, the star-light two hours old, the low water wearing a barely wrinkled calm, and the Chief puts our johnboat over the bulkhead. If we have sharp eyes and speed and luck, the boat will become a creel containing many future suppers. It's already a river-going pack mule, bearing a heavy-duty twelve volt battery to power the flounder light, which is a sealed bulb at the end of an aluminum pole. We could climb aboard ourselves—Miss Carrie, lady that she was, surely did her floundering from the dry confines of a boat. But with clothing clinging intimately to our bodies, we wade, seduced by the water's coolness on a humid night. The Chief grips the light-pole like an oversized baton in his left hand. His right hand holds a homemade gig, a slender, four-foot steel rod tipped on one end with a blunt point. Fancier gigs may be bought—gigs mounted on poles of any length, barbed gigs, gigs shaped like streamlined arrowheads or miniature tridents. Barbs have the advantage of keeping a flounder impaled while it's being hoisted into a boat; the Chief must put a hand beneath his speared quarry lest it slip off the gig and slide away.

Because I turn into a pumpkin, orange and useless, if I don't go to bed before midnight, I'm not often a member of the floundering party. I've gone often enough, however, to know that my eyes are not keen to see lurking flounder and that I'm capable of gigging not a fish but my own foot. The Chief usually sets off into the water with Al or Tom or Jim. And I think that, though the sport is hardly forbidden to women, male camaraderie takes a starring role in the exercise, just as it does for the cronies who perch in lawn chairs to surfcast in the river. I bid the men farewell and "Break a leg" and watch them wade out in the regulation dress of jumpsuits, sneakers, and baseball caps.

The sealed light is plunged beneath the water, a tiny sun casting more brightness on the river bottom than daylight ever could. The water looks like consommé, brown and transparent. Towing the boat, they walk slowly to the sandbar at the creek and the shoals beyond. The flounder come inshore at night to lie in hungry ambush; they flip sand or mud over the exposed sides of their dark-mottled bodies and rush out suddenly to seize their food—shrimp and smaller fish—in bulldog jaws. As for the predators on two legs, the Chief says this: "When the water washes in, it ripples the sand. You look for a break in the ripples, a break with a flat, oval shape. It may be a flounder—it is if you see the eyes, or it may just mark the track where a flounder was lying moments ago. But when you see it—*hit!*" As many phantoms are gigged as flounder, and sometimes the party comes home with little more than tales of newly vacated tracks or big ones scared off by a sneaker ill-placed on their topsides. But three or four keepers will do nicely, thank you. Sometimes, though, the bottom of the boat is heaped. Once the Chief and Al landed twenty plus one and followed that act on the next night with seventeen, a winter's worth of flounder for each family.

With gigging, as in any kind of planned fishing, success depends on skill and intuition and at least a tad of unintentional cooperation from the species sought—that it actually be, for example, in its accustomed haunts rather than off on vacation. But one or more times a year, on an early morning in the sultriest of weather, the tables are turned: we do not hunt out flounder, they seek us. Or they seem to, crowding the shallows by the bulkheads, casting themselves with abandon on the beaches, in the phenomenon known as a capital-J Jubilee. The event is local; we may hear of a Jubilee two miles upriver or across the water on the far shore but see none of it along the Point's margins. Or, it may happen here, on a half-mile stretch, but nowhere else. Out come the long-handled gigs, the ones that can reach seven feet, from the waist of a person standing on a bulkhead to the river's bottom where the flounder swarm. Every last soul cruises the bulkheads gigging flounder after flounder or scooping them up with bare hands. The wheelbarrows needed to cart them away are hardly mythic, for barrowloads are landed in the four or so hours that the Jubilee lasts. Every cooler is brought into service; refrigerators are raided for ice, and people caught short drive the twelve miles out to the Mom-and-Pop store and its ice machine. The cleaning tables shine with mica scales, run red with blood for the rest of the day. Freezers fill quickly. In a sense, the flounder have reversed the lemmings' run, leaping not into the sea but into air.

It's air they're gasping for. When the water is low and still and seems barely to flow, when no rain has fallen for days and the upper air wraps us in a hot wet blanket, when algae feed on run-off nutrients and bloom, the river can lose the dissolved oxygen needed by its animals. Without cool water and aerating whitecaps, without the wind that makes the water foam, the river is dead. Unable to breathe, the animals suffocate. Flounder is not the only species that suffers anoxia. Dead fish, from croaker to sea robins, rise and float on the surface. Shrimp, too, make Jubilee, and so do the blue crabs. The crabs give a day's warning of the event, for when the oxygen content of the water decreases to a dangerous low, they begin to scramble as best they can up the vertical walls of the bulkheads, and they do not crawl into baited pots but cling in hordes, like shipwrecked sailors, to the outsides of the wire cages.

The flounder's misfortune is our feast. I marvel, however, at the popularity of flounder flesh when so many others
of the river's fish are equally delectable. One syllogism to account for flounder-lust might be put this way: Flounder are
filleted, fillets have no bones, bonelessness is much to be desired when eating fish and, therefore, flounder are to be desired. But we also fillet bluefish, mullet, and other species.
Flavor seems to be a criterion; blues are "oily" and bottom-
feeding mullet "muddy," while flounder "don't taste like
fish." All fish have subtle flavors that can be fully savored
only when the fish is transferred immediately from water to
cleaning table to cooking fire. Might unconscious snobbery
play a part in the preference for flounder? Barring salmon, it's
the priciest fish in any market, though by the time it's sat in
the counter for a day or two, it tastes like any other well-aged
fish. I, too, relish flounder, but other fish more powerfully
raise my appetite, including some that bring the Point's almost unanimous, "Yuck!"

River TV, morning edition: Engines throbbing softly, a forty-
foot trawler motors into the Rounding just upstream of Courts
Creek. Midsummer sunlight bounces off its spanking white
paint as it closes inshore, almost to the first line of commercial
crabpots. Three small workboats, pale yellow and light blue
and white, are anchored there. A bare-chested man, waist-
deep in water, holds onto an upright pole that seems thrust
solidly into the river's bed. Three men in soaked t-shirts stand
fifty feet farther offshore; one of them holds a similar pole.
Between the poles, corks dancing on the water indicate that a
net lies below. When the trawler comes alongside the three
men, someone on deck puts the end of a net over a bar at the
trawler's stern and pushes the fabric into the water. Waiting
hands fasten it quickly to the second pole. And the trawler
turns, heading toward mid-river. As it chugs outward, the net
contained in the hold slides over the bar. Every hundred
yards, an electric-orange float bobs on the corkline. The Chief

and I count them—five, six, eight. The trawler has laid nearly half a mile of net.

"It's doing a long haul," The Chief says. "Gonna clean out the Rounding for sure. We won't catch fish coming down-river for the next couple of days."

The trawler turns back toward shore and pulls the far end of the net in its wake. Shouting, laughing, lighting occasional cigarettes, the men in the water wait. They're about to have company. Curiosity rampant, I shuck my land-clothes, pull on a jumpsuit, splash into the river, and start sloshing upstream.

As the trawler nears shore, it has pulled the net into a great half circle and begins to take it back onboard. When the net is nearly stowed, the waiting, bantering men spring into action unfastening the end of the long net and attaching two stout draw-lines to cleats on the trawler's gunwales. The sound of the engines becomes lower and more resonant as the trawler puts on power, pulls the lines taut, and keeps pulling. Two men uproot one pole from the river bottom and wade it toward the other pole. The net between the poles is made of three-quarter-inch mesh, far finer than that of the three-inch gill net now back in the hold. I see what's being done: the fine seine net is being drawn into a pocket that will contain the fish herded in by the coarser mesh. By the time I reach the men, the circle of the seine is closed. And the trawler keeps pulling the lines to draw the pocket's bottom inescapably tight.

No need for introductions. The men have positioned themselves around the seine's perimeter, and each uses both hands to hold the corkline above water. One tells me to grab onto a section of corkline, and I do. The encircled water flashes with fish—Spanish mackerel with pale orange polkadots on their sleek silver bodies, snub-nosed Florida pompano dipped in gold, a few jack crevalle, the inevitable croaker, and uncountable triangular wings that flap with great energy and churn the other fish in the net. The long haul has

121

scooped in dozens of stingrays, all of them the cow-nosed kind with two blunt protruberances at the end of each snout. We keep holding the corkline well above water. Only a few fish jump to freedom.

When the seine net is tight, the trawler returns to the impoundment. Two men scramble aboard and use large dip-nets to convey the catch piecemeal to wooden crates on the deck. The rays, however, are not saved but gigged and dropped back into the water, their muscular bodies and barbed tails landing right beside our relatively unprotected legs. One of the men still in the water wears shorts and has bare feet. He looks at me and says, "Nah, don't worry. They ain't gonna hurt nobody."

"People say they taste pretty good. Ever tried one?" I ask.

"Nah," he says, but the man with the gig calls, "You want one, we'll get you a nice one." Discarding the smaller rays, he selects one with a wingspan of two and a half feet, amputates its dangerous tail with a piratical-looking machete, and puts it in a burlap potato sack produced from somewhere on the trawler's crowded deck. He drops the filled sack overboard. I catch it and tow it behind me as I wade home. As I leave, the seine net still holding many fish has become just light enough to hoist aboard. The men grunt with effort as they haul it in. And the trawler, accompanied by the work-boats, departs so that the catch will reach the seafood market before the sun starts westering.

I don't know anyone on the river or elsewhere who has sampled stingray. This one is for Bonnie, who remarked off-handedly one day that those things had to be good or seafood restaurants couldn't get away with taking a biscuit-cutter to the wing meat, frying it up, and serving it straight-faced as "scallops" to unsuspecting customers.

Stingrays have no bones. Like their relatives, the equally flat but barbless skates and the torpedo-shaped sharks, their bodies are built on frames of cartilage, a structural design evolved well before the rise of the bony fishes. Many of the rays, including the cow-nosed variety, frequent shallow water and prowl the bottom to gather small molluscs and crustaceans that they grind against the horny plates in their mouths. If the evidence in the seine net is to be believed, the river teems with rays. They summer in the Rounding; in spring and fall, we see their great schools moving, dark wingtips boiling across the water. Wading for fun or to fish the net, we often step on flounder that give a sudden flip and scoot away. But we've never, hallelujah, set unwary foot on a stingray. Depending on the species, rays wear their barbs in various stations on their tails; the cow-nosed kind tucks its slightly curved thorn close to the place at which tail meets body. But, like the rattlesnakes and copperheads that call the Point home, the rays' first inclination is toward escape and peaceful coexistence.

I reach the wooden steps leading from the water to our front yard. Oof! The potato sack is heavy! Water has supported its weight on the way home. Now it's all I can do to heft the sack ashore. The Chief lifts it, sets it on the cleaning table, and estimates the ray's weight at twenty-five to thirty pounds. The sack heaves and slaps the table. The ray is still flexing its muscles with great vigor, though blood from its wound streams red and copious across the table's white surface. I race to Bonnie's house. "We've got something for you. Come see! Come see!"

"Oh, m'goodness," is all she can say. And she runs home to fetch a stainless steel basin to hold the meat.

Though he's never before dressed out a ray, the Chief has read about the procedure. Like an operating-room assistant, I hand him his knives. He makes a longitudinal cut at the point that the wings—really overdeveloped pectoral fins—join the ray's round torso. Then, knife held horizontally, he fillets outward along the tough white cartilage that runs from the body through the center of each fin. Dark-skinned on the dorsal side, creamy white on the belly, each

123

fin yields two fat steaks. The Chief skins them and puts them in Bonnie's basin. It's important to dress out a ray as soon as possible after capture because, like shark's meat, its flesh becomes contaminated by urea after death. Bonnie takes the fillets home to refrigerate them in a light brine that will prevent any lingering ammoniac taste.

She and Al summon us the next day for testing. Bonnie has sliced the steaks into long strips and sautéed them in browned butter judiciously seasoned with garlic. The Chief employs Bonnie's favorite dead pan word to pronounce judgment: "Outstanding." He reaches for more, and so do we all. The meat is dark. It looks and tastes like a mild beef, like cube steak become miraculously tender rather than furnishing an exercise in chewing leather. I echo the accolade: "Outstanding." Al nods agreement.

No one could mistake this meat for scallops. It does not mimic the shellfish in color, texture, or flavor. The ray's close cousin the skate may have been used by a restaurant looking to cut costs, but we have no confirmation of the rumor. Ray deserves its own place on a menu. What a pity that ray is unconventional fare not hallowed by advertising and a place in the supermarket.

I conclude the Grand Stingray Experiment by calling the seafood market to let the long-haul crew know that stingray is not just food but a gourmet's treat. The man on the phone's other end replies politely, but his tone implies that he thinks the lady is weird.

Now I lay claim to at least one large ray a year from Tom's flounder net. Those as big as the one brought to Bonnie yield eight to ten pounds of a no-beef beef that's blessedly free from sharp, sneaky bones and costs nothing but a little time and labor. And we've occasionally invited guests to dine on "seafood surprise." No one has yet bolted from the table when the truth was told. In fact, some people have asked for seconds.

*   *   *

Despite our best persuasions and our garlic-buttered samples, cow-nosed rays have never been acceptable as trade goods. People aren't hungry enough, as a rule, to be adventurous. As a medium of exchange, flounder of course rates exceptionally high, and higher still, at the very top of the list, the meat of *Callinectes sapidus*, the beautiful swimmer that tastes mighty good.

Acquiring crabmeat keeps me off the streets and out of trouble summerlong. Crabbing starts with the pots that nor'casters rip loose from commercial lines and cast up on the sands at the far side of the creek. The pots are cubes, two feet to a side, of plastic-coated wire that looks like chicken wire but of heavier gauge. Each pot is divided midway into two stories, the lower fitted with two (sometimes more) wide entrance sleeves and a bait compartment. Crabs seek their freedom by clambering into the upper story, but there they wait until the top closure is unfastened and they're shaken out, thudding into the container of the crabber's choice. The one or two pots I salvage upriver each year are lugged home across the creek and through the woods.

Usually, they're battered, and the Chief repairs them by joining gaping seams with metal rings and by making new top closures from hooks attached to newly scissored lengths of uncracked innertubing. The rings were never meant for mending crabpots; they're hog rings originally destined for clipping in pigs' nostrils to keep them from rooting under the fences that enclose their yards. When the pots are mended, the Chief's job is done. Since living under the ripe and penetrating smog of a Chesapeake crabcake factory in his early Navy days, he has disdained crab. He may be the only man in the world who does so.

The jobs of catching and processing are up to me. I bait the pots with menhaden or gizzard shad and toss them off the bulkhead while leaving onshore the white marker-floats, another gift from the river, that are attached to the pots by long lines of hemp or nylon. When the time for harvest comes, it's easy work—and dry—to grab the floats and haul the pots up and over the bulkhead. Brandishing and snapping their claws, the contents clatter into one of those hold-all five-gallon buckets. With stainless tongs, I sort them, grasping and flinging back all the jennies and those jimmies that measure fewer than the lawful five inches spine to spine. Though crabs can come in giant sizes—seventeen-inchers have been caught up-river on lines baited with chicken necks, seven-inchers are about the largest that can clamber sideways through the pots' entrance sleeves. Along with the jennies and the little ones, some of those seven-inchers are also returned to the river—those with snowwhite bellies, those whose carapaces give a hollow thunk when tapped lightly by the tongs. They've molted recently; their flesh, once crammed in too-small shells, is thin and stringy now, as if the furnishings of a studio apartment had been moved into a three-bedroom house. Seldom do I find a softshell, wobbly as jelly and defenseless, but when I do, its name is invariably Lunch. We could start a small-scale shedding operation—I've learned to tell the crabs called busters from those that are weeks away from their next molt, but the softshell harvested at random is that much more succulent for being rare. The hard crabs in the bucket may be declawed and cleaned raw, their shells tugged off, their gills and guts removed before they're cooked, or they may be steamed to fiery redness before the cleaning starts. And when they're cooked, I pick—and pick and pick. How intricate, how full of chambers and mazy hallways is the inner anatomy of a crab! When I was new at picking, I often lost my way, nor was there any thread to lead me from the labyrinth. Now, the map of crabby convolutions in my head, the bowls fill rapidly with meat, a bowl for firm white backfin, a bowl for smaller morsels, and a bowl for the clawmeat. The job satisfies in the way that weeding a garden or painting a wall can satisfy: with each uprooted clump of grass, each stroke of the roller, each tiny flake of meat that falls into a bowl, one sees results.

Crabpots deliver far more than the crabs they're meant to catch. Pinfish, feisty and flapping, are a daily certainty in the summerlong crabbing season; back to the river they go. Supper-sized striped mullet also invade the pots; their fate is the cleaning table. Flounder stow themselves on the wire pot-bottoms; most are fifty-dollar throw-backs. Several times each summer, a small, edible, and vocal species presents itself, decorated in the fantastic fashion of its tribe with iridescent turquoise stripes and orange freckles; it's a hogfish, the river term for French grunt, grinding its teeth to make the soft stridulations that give this grunt and many others in its family their common name. Once I pulled up a miniscule black sea bass. And once, an inch-long twig dropped from a pot onto the sand. I picked it up, and the twig curled itself into an S: a sea horse.

Why does a crabpot attract fish? For the bottom-feeders, like mullet and flounder, it's a misadventure placed squarely on their usual browsing grounds, or perhaps it's seen as a shelter, one that too often becomes as lethal as a killer-net if weary crabbers do not regularly pull their pots. For the sea horse, the wire may have been a substitute for the waterweed to which the species often clings with coiled tail. For other fish, the crabpot is a cafeteria: here's food neatly packaged in the bait compartment, help yourselves. Hauling in the pots provides as much suspense as fishing the net.

June through September, till the inshore water gains an autumn chill and the crabs migrate to deeper, warmer climates in the mud, I pick and I pick. Pound after pound, the trade goods stack up in the freezer. I've exchanged crabmeat for typewriter repairs and for an afghan big enough to cover our double bed on January nights. And backfin meat, the most coveted part of a crab yet the easiest to pick, affords us celebrations on those rare evenings that we gussy up and go out to dine. At summer's end I hand my pounds of backfin to the chef of an elegant restaurant inland; he waits for it because, unlike the backfin sold by the wholesalers, it's clean, not cluttered with fragments of mouth-stabbing shell. He hands me a receipt. The Chief and I shall splendidly indulge ourselves, Chateaubriand and wine. When the check is presented, with a satisfied flourish we simply sign our names.

A crabpot introduces me to sea serpents.

Crabs relish gizzard shad. I've experimented with bait from bluefish carcasses to chicken necks, but above all other lures, crabs are seduced by whole, fresh, strongly aromatic gizzard shad. So is that half-pint serpent better known as the American freshwater eel. In high summer, when I haul a pot, one or more foot-long, grey-green critters with the circumference of a fat cigar will slither through the mesh and drop— splash!—back into the briny before the pot is safely landed. Rarely, one of these small eels lands on terra firma. I used to flip them back into the river with my foot or with the tongs used for catching escaped crabs.

Sneak thieves! Bait pirates! Crabs and other fish are much too large to slink through the fine mesh that encloses bait, but slender eels just ooze right in and and gorge themselves. What good are they? Bonnie has eaten eel, and so has Tom's fishing friend Burt. Both allow separately, without collusion, that it tastes all right, but watch out, eat it all at one sitting. Why? "I'll tell you why," Bonnie says. "If you stash leftover eel in the fridge overnight, it turns raw." And Burt tells me on another day that his mother once fed him fried eel for supper but he hasn't touched it since because "I seen the dish she put in the icebox—that eel was settin' in a pool of blood." An old wives' tale surely, but I don't dispute the gospel according to Bonnie and Burt. I have, however, read a long shelf of cookbooks to learn ways of preparing the river's bounty. From Izaak Walton on, the authors agree unanimously that eel flesh is delicious and well worth the minutes and muscle needed to clean this fish that looks not like a fish but something that might have offered an apple to Eve. Taste buds that take to stingray can surely handle the "little snake with beaked nose," plain English for the scientific *Anguilla rostrata*. I want to try one.

Odd creatures, eels—as idiosyncratic in history as they are in appearance. They're sexual recluses, intrepid and determined long-distance travellers, and alchemists that transmute an originally transparent state to yellow and then to gleaming silver. They are not even remotely related to snakes. My ancient Greeks believed that eels were the product of earth's guts, generated spontaneously by springtime sun and rain out of river muck. And the idea has persisted till fairly recently that freshwater eels were indeed exceptions to the rule of sexual reproduction in finfish. The reasons for this notion were that nobody had caught them in the act nor did there appear to be any spawning grounds. No one has yet seen them breeding, but the riddle of where they do so was solved early in the present century—the Sargasso Sea. From there the larval eels, looking not like eels but tiny bits of cellophane, journey north and west for a year and some months. When they reach America's continental shelf, they begin the metamorphosis into the miniature but recognizable eels known as elvers. And they head inland, swimming by day when the moon is dark, by night when it reaches full bloom, up the estuaries and brackish rivers into freshwater streams and ponds. As they move farther away from their natal ocean, their bodies make massive physiological adjustments from the salty environment to one that's salt-free. In the decade-plus that it takes them to reach sexual maturity and head home for the Sargasso, they can travel astonishing distances. Some make their way as far as the Mississippi, and some go in for mountaineering, ascending into waters flowing more than a mile above sea level. They can even travel overland for short distances, up dry spillways and over dew-soaked fields, because the mucus coating their bodies prevents loss of moisture. And as they move onward and upward, the alchemy takes place. The see-through babies become freckled with color and finally gain the complete pigmentation known as "yellow." Their backs range in color from greeny-grey to near-black; yellow refers to the sulphury sheen on their pale bellies. For the next ten years they'll feed and grow and turn at last to sexually mature silver adults. The feeding ceases then, the bodies now a yard or more in length will readapt to salt water, and the eyes of the females will bulge huge and round like the eyes of Byzantine madonnas. They will complete their circle, going home to the Sargasso where they will breed and die.

Learning these details of their history is the direct result of a wrestling match. Early on a bright June morning, I go to the bulkhead and begin to haul the crabpots. One contains five clacking jimmies, a flounder too small to keep, and an eel—an eel just small enough to have slid through the pot's wide entrance sleeve but much too large for any get-away through the pot's mesh sides. It is as long and big around as a husky woman's forearm.

I holler for the Chief, who is sitting peaceably at the kitchen table to wake up over his first cup of coffee. Alarmed, he bursts from the trailer onto the deck. "What's wrong?"

I point at the eel. "Help!"

He comes running. "My gawd," he says respectfully. "It's the Loch Neuse monster."

It is a challenge, too, a huge and thrashing invitation to test the praises of cooks from Izaak Walton on. How, exactly, are we to deal with a sea serpent? The cookbooks give advice: stun the creature with a whack on its spine, nail its head to a tree, make a circular cut just aft of the pectoral fins, peel back the tough skin and yank it off with a pair of pliers. The eel, limp and naked, is then to be gutted in the usual fashion, cut into two- or three-inch rounds, and cooked according to chef's fancy. We obey these violent instructions, though I do not cut super-eel in chunks but fillet it into thick ribbons of boneless flesh. Breaded and sautéed, it is as advertised: delicious. The firm white meat has the texture of chicken and the taste of— what? Something light, almost sweet, with only the most delicate hint that eel comes from the sea. Is such a treat, though, worth the bashing, the outright brutality used to obtain it?

Wrong-headed, the advice in those cookbooks! Have the authors ever followed their own directions? Or have they simply gone to a handy-dandy fish market to purchase eels already "subdued"—one author's word—by someone else? I still wince remembering the treatment doled to super-eel.

And I still go eeling, for there are methods I can live with. Because crabpots are chancy at best for catching sea serpents, we've acquired eelpots of a sturdy shoe-box type, two feet long and a foot square, built of fine-mesh wire. Eels prowl mostly at night; the pots are set at dusk, their marker-floats resting on dry land, and hauled the next morning. In summer, prime season for inshore eeling, a single pot sometimes delivers as much as I can heft—twenty writhing pounds of *Anguilla* intricately tangled in the living equivalent of a Gordian knot. A few tails thrust themselves through the mesh and work vigorously back and forth—an eel uses its stern extremity as a pry bar—but the efforts are futile. I empty the catch into a forty-eight-quart cooler and sort it by hand, first removing the tag-alongs, the tiny crabs and toadfish, the inevitable pinfish. No overkill: I let the foot-long cigars go and keep only the one or two arm-sized eels that we can use. The hand that sorts them wears a cotton glove, not for protection—eels for all their fearsome looks don't bite—but for ease in handling the catch. Slippery as an eel—the dead simile squirms to life under the force of literal truth. Try to pick up an eel with a bare hand. Sorting eels, the glove quickly becomes coated with mucus. For better purchase, I spread my gloved palm on the ground and use the mucus as glue to pick up sand. After sorting, the keepers are sprinkled with ordinary table salt. In fifteen minutes they are docile. Quick hosing removes the mucus. It's not hard, then, to slit the skin, loosen its edges, and peel it back with one hand gripping the eel's head and the other, closed around its body, pulling sternward with a swift stripping motion. I fillet all our eels; no sense bothering with spongy bones like those in chicken wings. The meat is used immediately or frozen to last well into winter, long after the eels migrate offshore in early October.

What good is an eel? Good for supper! And they have their other human uses. Angling for something less snake-like for dinner, the finicky may cut them in small pieces and put them on the business end of a fishing pole. Eelskin with its tiny, deeply embedded scales may be tanned into a thin, supple, tough leather that outlasts the stitches used to make it into belt or hatband or billfold. To tan the skins, one traditional but not outdated recipe calls for them to be marinated for a fortnight in urine. I haven't tested it, but I might to make an eelskin thong like that used once upon a time by Cherokee women in the belief that their long hair would grow even longer if it were tied back with such a magical fastening.

I've learned enough, too, about the eel's internal anatomy to know why cooked eel turns "raw" after it's been stored in the refrigerator overnight. As pearl accretes around a grain of sand, a folk-belief grows around a small but irritating nub of fact that needs somehow to be explained. But the experts I approached, Fisheries' specialists in seafood cookery, had never heard of such a belief, nor could they suggest its source. They did, however, mail me a pamphlet full of recipes. Hands-on experience at the cleaning table provided the fact I was looking for: improper cleaning. Unlike croaker, seatrout, and most other fish in the river, the innards of an eel do not stop at the anal opening but extend an inch or more tailward. There its kidney lurks, dark red and waiting to stain leftovers if it's not removed.

On summer nights, in the light from the cleaning table, we see eels nosing at the remains of the fish we've just dressed. They're meat-eaters, rejecting carrion but taking the rest of what the river offers, from live crustaceans to fresh carcasses. Like the crepuscular armies that swarm into office buildings with mops and brooms, eels are a cleaning crew, providing prompt, efficient service to the waters they inhabit.

Sea serpents—*Anguilla* did not itself directly inspire tales of such creatures. It's not ocean-going nor monstrous enough to have so kindled the imaginations of old-time mariners and caused them to mark vast stretches of unexplored ocean with the legend *Hic dracones*—Here be snakes. The river holds more than meets the eye, and in the river anything might happen. Eels in their strangeness hint at marvels hidden in the salty deeps and shallows. I think I believe in sea serpents.

Our grandson Russell, not quite five, teeters on the bulkhead. He won't tumble into the river; his mother Lisa kneels on the grass beside him, her arm around his small, lean belly. He is learning to work a spinning rod, one made to fit a child's hands and abilities. A chunk of menhaden dangles from the hook. Cast, reel in, cast again, he's awkward, giggling, but he's getting the idea.

Ignoring the commotion, Sally dozes on a sunny patch of pine straw. The Chief and I sit on the deck watching, wondering what, if anything, the small boy will catch. It's nearly suppertime; we shade our eyes and squint against the river's white-gold dazzle. Grandparents, mother, boy, we're all wishing with all our might that something will answer to the bait and strike, bending the rod, and stay hooked till the boy lands his first fish ever.

"Lost one," Lisa calls. "Now, Russell, when something hits the other end, you pull back quick, like this." She puts her hands on his and shows him how.

Our wishes grow so large they're almost palpable. But, according to the most authoritative legends, we're not supposed to utter them until the fish is caught and speaks: "Let me live, and I will grant your heart's desire."

The Brothers Grimm give report of the fisherman who

133

dwelled with his wife in a shanty by the sea. Day after day, year on year, he cast his line without much luck until the balmy morning that he pulled the prince of flounder from water that was calm and surpassing clear. And the fish offered the traditional bargain, "Your wishes come true in exchange for my life." The fisherman consulted his wife. She wanted a cottage, then a stone castle. The flounder acceded, but the sea, still calm, took on a dark opacity. She demanded to be king, then emperor, then pope. The waters twisted, giving off a stench; they turned black and bubbled as a brisk wind rose; they roared and boiled, waves crashing while thunder rumbled in the sky. When she wished to be God, lightning cracked, the pitch-black water roared, earthquakes shook the land and sea. And the flounder said to the fisherman, "Go home to your shanty."

No, that's not the ending that we with bated breath are angling for. All we want is a fish, one little fish. It may be, however, that the boy's luck will be that of the *Arabian Nights'* fisherman who cast his net four times into the sea. The first three tries brought in successively a dead jackass, a pitcher full of mud and sand, and a cultch of broken pottery and glass. The fisherman's fourth cast netted a copper jar, which he opened. A dense cloud steamed forth, gathering bulk until it materialized as a genie of superhuman size. Willing in the first four centuries of confinement to grant the dearest wishes of his liberator, he had become so cramped with rage at continuing imprisonment that he had sworn to kill whoever set him free. "You can do anything, can't you?" the fisherman said. "Anything and everything," the genie boasted. "But I doubt," said the fisherman, "that you can ever again make yourself small enough to fit in that jar." When rage had stuffed itself back into the jar, the fisherman clamped on the lid and fastened it tight.

A happy ending, if not the one we want for the fish story telling itself on the bulkhead. The river, though, might provide an *Arabian Nights'* catch of pottery, broken glass, and a beer can laden with sand. It might, I hope not, substitute a drowned cat for the jackass. But may all genies stay crouched forever in their copper prisons.

"I got one! I got one!" small boy shouts. His mother laughs gleefully and applauds. Dozing Sal bounds to attention. The Chief and I go running.

Pinfish. Its flapping body slaps the air. Wet scales reflect a rainbow of light. Lisa unhooks it and hands it to her son pointing out the dorsal-fin spines by which the fish earns its name. "Hold it just so, Russell. Don't get stuck." With a whoop, he sends the fish home. Fish hits the water and flips out of sight.

As it disappears, I see the ending to this afternoon's fairytale. Fish, allowing itself in belly-driven ignorance to be caught, has granted the boy's heartspoken wish. And boy has honored his part of the bargain by letting fish go free. Yet, something is still on the hook, the boy has swallowed the bait, and it won't let him go. He'll leave the salty river and return to the cool, fresh inland streams and ponds of the midwest: bass and bream, crappie, perhaps someday a muskellunge. Before supper he catches another pinfish and releases it. The ending to this story is really a beginning.

The hours spent in fishing *are* deducted by the gods. They never let even the smallest of us get away. But fishing does convey one benefit quite apart from the pleasures of pursuit and dining amply on the catch. Fishing, we work on timeless river time, forgetting not only what day it is but the very fact that we are mortal. Concentration becomes so focused on the immediate that there's no brain-space for other, greyer thoughts. And that's reward enough.

6

Hurricane Gloria

BONNIE TELEPHONES. "You-all evacuating like everybody else?"

"Stay here if we can," the Chief replies.

She says, "Can't stay in your trailer, that's for sure. Put your trust in brick. Come bunk with us."

The river provides, and the river can put the fear of God in us. At breakfast-time, yesterday's hurricane watch was up-graded to a warning. Four days ago, a tropical depression un-folded its wet, grey umbrella over the Atlantic far to the south. Since then, the Point has stood under a fringe of rain, now sprinkling, now falling with a steady sozzle. Under the push of northerly winds, curling whitecaps have hissed across the immense reaches of the river. The water has risen to a level that nearly covers the old pier pilings off the Nay-Sayer's shore, pilings that usually protrude three feet above the sur-face. Water licks the webbed feet of the laughing gulls perched on these fragile posts. The temperature has fallen— blanket nights and sweater days. In the interludes between rain, Sal and I have walked our rounds: redstarts and black-and-white warblers pausing in the woods before they fly farther south; a pied-billed grebe, newly arrived for the winter, riding on the high water close inshore; snow geese, luminescent against grey evening skies, winging their way to the Sound. It's the season of autumn migrations and peak time for hurricanes. Records kept for the last hundred years, from 1886 to the present, show that the Point lies on that portion of the North Carolina coast with the second longest hurricane season and the highest incidence of devastating storms.

By noon yesterday, the tropical depression had earned a name that might have been uttered by dark angels, Gloria. *Gloria de profundis*, glory out of the deeps. Gathering speed, whirling like a carousel out of control, the storm's winds were clocked at 150 miles an hour. They spun dizzily, fatally, six hundred miles to the southeast working their way northwest toward Hatteras. Toward the Point. This morning's forecast tells coastal residents to expect landfall in twelve to eighteen hours. The exodus has begun. Joe, Lana, and their children have fled to town. Dorothy and Kent have hitched their Airstream trailer to the International station wagon and pulled inland. Of the dozen or so families living on the waterfront from our place to just downriver of the boat ramp, only two have chosen to challenge Gloria by staying put. A few more families, Mo and Joyce among them, Jim and Valerie moving in, stand fast, trusting that their dwellings are far enough inland to withstand an onslaught. The yard dogs have no choice; for them, it's sink or swim. They seem to know that heavy weather approaches, for they're lying low, snugged under left-behind pickup trucks or in the crawl spaces beneath the emptied houses. Sally won't let us out of her sight. She's a hazard, glued to our legs as we move inside and out to batten down. Where are yesterday's bright warblers, where the omnipresent gulls?

The Chief hauls our orange gill-net barrel behind the shed while I fold lawn chairs. All that can be irremediably kidnapped by wind and water is put away—garden hose, the rope hammock, the shovel stuck in the pile of fill dirt by the bulkhead. At mid-morning Al moseys across the drainage ditch. This time his baseball cap states that "Country folk can survive."

"Tell you what worries me most," he says. "Super-high water coming way over these bulkheads. I've seen it before, two feet, three feet, and I tell you we're gonna see it again."

Are we idiots to offer ourselves to the maw of a hurricane? Are we duped by the instinct that calls us to stay in our burrow? Bonnie's right that the trailer is no place to ride out a major storm, even though it's anchored in place with more straps than mandated in the county's code for mobile homes. Lesser winds than Gloria can snap cables as if they were dry twigs. If Al is right that super-high water will roll over the bulkheads and sweep the land, we face that possible damage, too. The water now thuds on the bulkhead wall two feet below its cap. A five-foot surge would turn the little azaleas in the front yard to marine vegetation. It would knock at the trailer's door and enter uninvited. We'll evacuate ourselves two doors downriver, to Bonnie and Al's brick fortress.

"Come over whenever you're ready," Al says, and he points at the river. "Well, will you look yonder!"

Bottle-nosed porpoises are rolling downriver. They're not moving in their usual dip-and-rise, single-file fashion. They're clustering, playing, standing on their heads and slapping their tails on the water.

The drizzle has thickened, settled into rain. Yard items stashed, we go inside. Sally climbs into a chair and curls her damp self into a ball. She doesn't doze but watches closely as we check the candle supply, the radio's batteries, and the propane canister for the Coleman lamp. We fill the canning kettle, the bathtub, and pots and pans with water. Ordinary afternoon thunder-boomers often disrupt the Point's power. No electricity: no heat for the stove, no refrigeration, no water pumped from the well and, thus, no flushing of toilets. What might a giant such as Gloria do? At 150 miles an hour, her punch exerts a pressure of 112 pounds per square foot, more than enough to turn iron skillets into lethal weapons, more than enough to unbury the dead. According to the news, we won't receive that full knockout blow, but pulverizing hundred-mile winds can be expected. And worse may be the storm surge—wind-driven water crashing over the land and using its broad frontal blade like a gargantuan plow to shove everything movable inland.

The Chief, hoping to keep its floorboards dry, moves his nearly antique Buick to slightly higher ground behind Bonnie and Al's sturdy bricks. In my car I pack valuables, the one-of-a-kind things whose loss would mean impoverishment: binoculars, typewriter, the hefty Greek lexicon, the texts and manuscript of the tragedy for which I'm trying to find English, the small looseleaf notebook holding twenty years of addresses and telephone numbers, the field guide containing the long list of birds seen at the Point. I drive to ground that Al pronounces truly water-safe, the entrance lane to Mo's barn. The rain begins to pelt as I walk home. The wind has calmed, though, and the face of the river is hardly ruffled.

By early afternoon, the wind begins to pick up, lathering the water with whitecaps. Bonnie calls to report a waterspout upriver above the Rounding. We see these marine tornadoes frequently in the hot months when afternoon thunderheads gather and roll down the far shore crackling with white fire and spitting rain. Waterspouts may dance in dervish escort to these storms. Their columns that connect water and sky are not made of salt water drawn up from the river but grow down from low-flying clouds as grey, whirling cords of freshly braided mist. Miles usually separate us from this phenomenon, but last year one column came spinning to our shore huge as a newly-liberated genie. It hunched itself and leaped over Bonnie's house to shear five stout branches from the mimosa by the back door. It vanished without further harm.

The river is shallow and in our portion, shore to five-mile-distant shore, nowhere much more than three fathoms deep. The shallowness can lead to trouble when the wind hauls suddenly. A gentle, southerly, eight-knot breeze will spin around, reappearing instantly as a fresh gale out of the north. It cracks its whip and drives water in from the Sound. The water, scraping along the shallow riverbed, has nowhere to go but up. Waves rise and grow white manes. And every year, such a conspiracy of wind and waves steals volition from sailors and redirects some of them willy-nilly to our shore. We've seen the whole Flying Scot flotilla of a children's summer camp across the river thwarted in its attempt to sail downriver to the fishing community of Oriental. Instead, the wind sent the fleet of twenty-foot sailboats at right angles to its intended course and pushed it due west, marooning a ruckus of teen-aged castaways in our yard. I asked the head counsellor why sail in such a wind, and he replied, "The challenge." On another day, a spring afternoon when the river still held a shivering chill, we watched one of these sudden gales tear a large sloop from her course along the far shore. In ten minutes flat, she was blown aground on the sandbar near the creek. The three-man crew leaped overboard and struggled for more than two spray- and wind-lashed hours to shove the hull off the embracing sands. We were ringside spectators, up to our gizzards in cold, slapping water to rescue our unsecured gill net that high waves had taken mere minutes to fling a hundred feet upriver.

We pack clothes, lantern, sleeping bags, and food, with kibble for Sally, in plastic sacks and tote them through dripping rain to our refuge. The lawn has become a shallow lake where grass and pine straw float like pondweed. Water rushes down the drainage ditches. The rising river punches at the bulkhead only a foot below the cap, and it already tongues the bottoms of piers as far as we can see downriver. Al's low pier is completely covered. The Chief's adrenalin flows fast; he's positively enjoying himself, eyes shining, energy at peak. I don't feel safe. I know that my sluggish human mechanisms are responding to the fall in barometric pressure, that my mind is alarmed by its inability to envision coming events, but it seems as if the clouds, the very air, thick with premature night, are pressing a sooty lid upon the world. We wolf an early supper at home and flee for quarters more secure. The world is pitch-black and howling. All the constellations are effaced. Just after the autumn equinox, at this time of evening we should have light. But no one tonight is issuing a *fiat lux*.

Bonnie's capacious kitchen-dining room—a great room, really—is a haven, warm with light and biscuit smells and human chatter. In this room I've helped slip the skins off scalded tomatoes destined for canning, and I've wielded a knife to bone tough, old rabbits destined for the sausage machine. Here Bonnie and I have taken on Al and the Chief in countless games of four-handed pinochle; sometimes, not often, we've won. Tonight Bonnie reaches over counters crowded with kettles, basins, buckets full of water, to hand plates of food to her daughters. Jake and Lolly sit with Al and the kids at the dining table. We pull up chairs while Sal does her Dobersneak on a cat crouched in a corner.

"No," Jake is bellowing. "We got to get on the road."

"You guys are nuts," says Al. "It's too late, too dark, too wet, too everything. There's a real bitch a-comin', let me tell you. Dumb!"

Bonnie obeys the commandment of neighborliness "C'mon, stay here. We've got plenty of room, the more the merrier. You can go as soon as Gloria blows over."

The cat spits and slaps Sally's nose hard enough to draw blood. Sal retreats under the table near Jake's feet. He ignores her, the first time he's ever ignored her, for he's busy shaking his head at Lolly as she tries to cajole him into delaying the journey for at least one night.

"No," he says. "Ain't no weather gonna slow me down. Arizona, here I come, where the hurricane don't ever show its ugly face."

"Stay," Bonnie begs.

"No."

"All I can say then is what you say to anybody making a trip on the high seas—bon voyage."

The wind rips around the house, rain pummels roof and windows, but off they go, Jake driving a van laden with household goods, Lolly at the wheel of an old black pickup pulling a U-Haul trailer. Take-off is momentarily delayed by the need to snug down the flapping tarp that covers chairs and boxes in the pickup's bed. Jake, after eighteen years on the river, is going home to his native desert. The four hundred rabbits were slaughtered or sold; the goats, geese, and scrawny ducks transported west weeks ago. Jake and Lolly will be back for one or two more loads. Al watches at the back door as van and truck lurch toward the mailboxes. The dirt road has become a slithery quagmire.

"Well, isn't this cozy," Bonnie says and pours a sip of peach schnapps all around. We lift our glasses to the vanishing tail-lights.

Everything that can be done to prepare for Gloria has been done. We wait. K.D. and her sisters joke and squabble and complain because television programs have been pre-empted by incessant bulletins. News clips of the day's events show bumper-to-bumper traffic inching over the bridge to Morehead City from the narrow and defenseless barrier island of Bogue Banks. Havelock and Cherry Point have declared a mid-evening curfew on vehicular traffic—not soon enough to stop Jake and Lolly on their pell-mell way west. Gloria's winds, though diminished, still revolve at better than a hundred miles an hour and are due to shriek onshore at Hatteras in three hours, in two. The decrease in wind-speed holds no comfort; Hatteras lies about sixty miles in a straight line northeast of the Point. And the nor'easter here is gaining force, buffeting the front of the house, screaming. The bricks deaden the sound of thumping wind as it strikes harder and more often. Yet, as if the wind needs time to catch its breath, lulls occur. Sally and Bonnie's white toy poodle race out to squat, and the human rest of us follow to observe the churning river.

Water spurts skyward over the top of Al's bulkhead, wooden like ours. Spindrift flies at us, along with rain blown horizontal. A fishing chair bolted mere moments ago to a pier three doors downriver rides upright toward the Rounding on white-maned, bucking waves.

"She's a doozy, all right," Al says, closing the door behind him and wiping the rain, the salt spray from his face with a plaid handkerchief. "Might be as bad as '33."

Bonnie says, "'33—when we first moved here that's all they used to talk about—how the old farm house was knocked down and swept away, how the dead cows got washed up in the trees, the waves were that high. People saved their chickens by putting them up in trees. They stood in a chain like a bucket brigade just passing those birds along. Then *they* climbed the trees. They talked about it and talked about it, the most humongous hurricane ever to hit this coast, and they kept talking till we got the hurricane of '70."

Al knows that storm by hearsay. "They tell me the water came up in '70 and rolled clear across the fields into the woods. Don't think we're gonna get that this time."

Bonnie says, "August, it was. I was staying with my folks, and when the wind died down, we put on water clothes and waded out to see how old Henry was doing. You know he only had one and a half legs. My folks' house was high enough so the water didn't come in, but we could look out and see water right up to the underside of Henry's old trailer—that tiny, falling-apart trailer with the built-on shack that still sits next-door to my folks. Trumpet vine is going to pull it down one of these days.

"We went in, and old Henry's floor was awash, water lapping around the kitchen-table legs, pushing at the rocker where Henry sat. And there he was, captaining his rocking chair and wearing a bright orange life jacket. He wouldn't, absolutely would *not*, let us take him to our house. 'Don't you worry,' he said. 'Just pick me up across the river when this storm blows out.' Feisty old man. We just let him be. When the storm stopped, I think he was a little disappointed to find himself in his own chair in his own house rather than fetching up yonder in Pamlico County."

Gloria's wind has unlatched the storm door between house and the front deck. It slams against closed wooden door and, hinges screaming, swings out to bang against the bricks. Crash, screech, rattle, bang, the rhythms are unpredictable, the sounds cacophonous, clashing cymbals, drumrolls, whistles, all orchestrated to insane crescendo by the wind. Rain blasts against the front windows; waves boom on the seawall. The lights in kitchen and living room still cast a warm brightness, and the television still sends out a steady babble telling us that we are now experiencing Gloria's full strength and that schools up and down the coast will be closed tomorrow. But K.D. and her sisters, who would usually make noisy, popcorn-eating, night-long celebration at such news, have been silenced by uncertainty and gone to bed. Sally dozes on the floor at the foot of the sofa-bed that's been assigned to the Chief and me in an alcove off the great room. In sleep, if sleep will come amid such pandemonium, there may be respite. I unroll my sleeping bag, and as I climb in, the power goes off. We all hold our breath. For a split second, I hear the human silence more clearly than the immane discord of the storm. Sleep does come, rocking me lightly; I drift on its surface hearing men's voices amid the shattering tumult. The wind drives rain between the wooden door and its frame; droplets of water land cold on my face. When the Chief comes to bed, I am completely unaware that he has joined me.

An internal alarm goes off. Time to rise. No, it's dark outside, or not quite dark, for the moon shines brilliant through the front windows and its near-full light makes shadows in the room. Aside from the Chief snoring softly, peacefully beside me, the only sound is no sound at all. The wire that held us tense and humming between heaven and earth has snapped and let us go.

144

At first light, the telephone—it works!—starts an incessant trill. Evacuees are calling: What's it look like at my place? Did my bulkhead hold? Have you seen my dog? We don't know anything yet, though Al estimates, accurately it turns out, that winds exceeding eighty miles an hour, more than minimum strength for a hurricane, have hammered the Point. Bonnie and Al's brick house stands intact except for the front storm door that hangs, twisted, from one hinge.

Gloria in excelsis! What a kind, golden day! It is as if Eden has risen like a phoenix out of Armageddon. Full sun and shirt-sleeve temperatures, with winds blowing strong out of the southwest. Sandbars spread themselves like broad-beamed bathers on both sides of the creekmouth. Shallow pools of water cover the yards like glistening mirrors.

Bonnie and I pull on boots and go out, Sal and Bonnie's little poodle romping around us. In good Point fashion, we accumulate another dog almost immediately. Jake's skittish cocker-cross emerges sodden from a den beneath his porch. We thought he'd taken both his small dogs to Arizona. Where is Mama-Dog, his curly-haired white mutt? The cocker-cross won't come near us but trails in our wake.

The day's beneficence makes it easier to survey the damage calmly as we make our way to Bonnie's parents' house. The telephone has let us know already that Mo and Joyce are safe. Upriver from the Point's boat ramp, not one pier stands, not the simple twenty-foot kind nor the long, elaborate ones with gazebos. The bulkheads—poured concrete, corrugated sheets of asbestos cement, salt-treated lumber, the material doesn't matter—have all fallen except for two, Bonnie and Al's and, thank goodness, ours. The bricks and cinderblocks used as backfill behind bulkheads are strewn, some whole, some crumbled to pebble-sized chunks, over the front yards. The wreckage looks like that of a bombed city. The surging waves have also cast pier-planking and driftwood copiously over yards and fields, and they have torn voraciously at shore that only yesterday was walled against the gouging waves.

Even we whose bulkheads still stand have lost soil. It will take 182 cubic yards of dirt to replace what the river took behind our bulkhead alone. Trees lie uprooted, including two red cedars planted thirty years ago by Tom's front door. Luckily, no trees have smashed down on anyone's cottage or trailer, but the gale has stolen one roof, and furniture squats drenched beneath open sky. We can see how far inland the storm surge swept by the salt-blackened leaves of myrtles and azaleas and by the flotsam left as the water receded—splintered boards, strips of filter cloth and scraps of light blue vinyl used to line bulkheads, aluminum trailer-skirting, all manner of plastic garbage from detergent containers to a royal blue milk crate. At the water's farthest reach, heaps of pine straw lie in an irregular line like high-tide wrack on a beach. The water has risen and flooded over the waterfront lots, over the tier immediately behind, across the dirt lane down which Jake and Lolly slithered last night, and into the fallow fields almost to the tree line—three-tenths of a mile.

Breakfast awaits at Bonnie's parents' house. How friendly Joyce's kitchen is—wooden cabinets glowing warm, walls decorated with small, handmade baskets of wicker, split oak, and braided grass. "Sit right down," Joyce says. "Here's something I baked just a little bit ago. It sure helps to have a gas stove when the power goes out." We settle gladly into Miss Carrie's mahogany chairs, and she hands us paper plates holding large wedges of pineapple upside-down cake. Bonnie takes a bite and delivers her standard encomium, "Outstanding."

At our place, the storm has raged gently. It threw dead branches like jackstraws over the grass and buried the little front-yard azaleas with pine straw. At water's edge it took away the fish-cleaning table and the wooden steps leading down to the river. At the trailer it shoved the skirting underneath at a forty-five-degree angle. But the floor inside is dry! So is the Chief's old Buick. Mine did not fare so well; parked well above water's reach at Mo's barn, it has fallen victim to the wind. A stout branch rests like a balance beam across its roof; the impact has made an expensive dent. But the car's irreplaceable contents are safe. I drive them home.

Battery-powered radios report that Gloria, after making landfall at Hatteras, is whirling full-tilt up the coast still causing havoc. By mid-morning the Point swarms with people, strangers come to rubberneck or to inquire about lost dogs, residents returning for the clean-up. The storm has shredded schedules and made nonsense out of clocks and calendars. The brick house has become command headquarters, gathering information and dispersing it on that life-line telephone. The electric company has sent a representative to check damage; he tells us that we'll be without power for another day or two. Bonnie and the kids sweep the neighborhood collecting perishable food from dark refrigerators, and Al builds a hearty fire in the woodstove. Tonight, there'll be hot food for hungry bellies. Bonnie puts out kibble for Jake's cocker-cross, which still skulks wistfully on the fringes of our comings and goings. White Mama-Dog has not yet reappeared.

In the afternoon I run an obstacle course through the woods to the creek. The Nay-Sayer has lost another ten feet of land right next to our line. Five slender loblollies and a sweet-gum I couldn't put my arms around have toppled into the river, and the woods path is nearly impassable because of fallen trees and the prickly curtains of greenbriar they pulled with them when they crashed down. The moribund pine that held the pileated woodpeckers' nest has been truncated. Unnatural debris also chokes the woods—lumber, pieces of bulkheading, pier planks, telephone-pole pilings, a set of steps in excellent condition. I go slowly onward climbing over deadfalls, crawling under trees still green but pushed over by the storm's blast. At woods' end a tumble of uprooted bear-grass yuccas litters the beach, and the storm-impelled river has broached several small channels into the pond. The beach has moved inland over the needlerushes that guard the pond's perimeter. The creek itself flows through a channel three times wider than it was yesterday.

The wild places will repair themselves in their own good time. The places that people have tried to tame will not wait. The music that will characterize the weeks to come starts this very afternoon—calling voices, hammers, chainsaws, pumps sucking sand and clay out of the riverbed so that new bulkhead pilings can be sunk deep. Tom and Merle arrive with fishing friends to begin clearing away the rubble that conceals their grass and clogs the drainage ditch. Kent retrieves much of his bulkhead from the woods; owners seem to know their own lumber as intimately as they know their children and their dogs. In milder storms, the nor'easters that simply send the water spilling ankle-deep over bulkheads, people have stood on their lawns amid swirling foam and tossed out anchor-weighted lines to snag pier-sections as they plunge by. The salvaged lumber is placed out of water's reach, and the owners are notified. Now, boats go empty into the creek and come back heaped to the gunwales with usable boards, some of them familiar, some from unknown piers and bulkheads down the river. When it comes to piers, a lesson has been learned. Replacing elevated models, many of the new ones are being built low over the river so that rising water will sweep over them rather than deliver steady rabbit punches to their underbellies. Part of what the storm has taken, the storm replaces; the set of steps found in the woods will soon be attached to our bulkhead. All hands turn to restoration, picking up tools and pounding away or gathering acres of trash and taking it to the dump in a steady procession of pickups. People give help freely, gladly, where help is needed. Bonnie feeds exhausted multitudes with her take from the neighborhood refrigerators—meatloaf, eggplant with cheese, creamed cauliflower, biscuits with leftover gravy, a corn-tomato-okra gumbo, green peppers simmered with onions. For something sweet, she provides an applecake. On the third day, the day that crews from South Carolina mend our power lines, she reports good news. Jake has called in from Missouri and learned that his bulkhead is smashed, his pier is gone, his front yard chewed in half, but the cocker-cross is eating though avoiding people. But Mama-Dog. . . .

"Would've served that damn dumb cocky right, get washed away. It wouldn't get in for the ride," he roared. "But Mama-Dog, she's with me in the van."

For Mama-Dog's sake, if not for Jake's, we rejoice. We've been hanging back the way the cocker-cross hangs back, but now we can say the word aloud—drowned—because we know she isn't.

When Jake returns three weeks later to pick up another load of household goods for transport west, he provides a coda to Gloria's hit-and-run. Clad in jeans and a t-shirt with a hole neatly centered on his belly button, he stands haunch-deep in water to survey the damage done to his homestead. Nothing of his seawall remains; if pieces have been recovered, they're probably incorporated now into somebody else's re-building project. The pilings, walers, and tongue-in-groove boards for a new bulkhead lie stacked on the ground beside his cottage. Debris litters the water around Jake's feet—the concrete blocks and slick tires that he's used to augment, and reduce the cost of, fill dirt. He looks upriver: Dorothy sows seed on newly replaced earth, Al splits the trunks of downed trees for firewood, Merle rakes up the last of the rubble. He looks downriver: Kent and crew put runners and planks on a new pier. In desultory fashion, Jake hoists a fallen block from the water, heaves it ashore, and steps back to peer again at the bustle on either side. He's moving slowly, waiting for an offer of help. He has, after all, helped Kent install a new bulkhead, and he's leased his bull strength to other heavy en-terprises. The catch is that he has always held out his palm to be crossed with silver. So, for three days, Jake stands forlorn and silent in the water. The river is calm; his bulkhead could have been nearly replaced in this time, by now he could have been loading his van with cartons, furniture, and a bathtub for his ducks. Eager though we are to lift a toast to departing tail-lights, no one lends aid, no one even speaks except in passing. On the fourth day, he opens his mouth and his wallet. Reconstruction begins.

Thunk-clunk, we load another wheelbarrow with the concrete pebbles and blocks of brick that litter Tom and Merle's yard. Seven of us have cleared the debris from shore almost to the cottage steps. Downriver, Al and Kent are standing in waist-high water to wrestle broken bulkhead timbers ashore. A little farther down, a crew installs a new roof on the shorn cottage. Everyone is joking, laughing, wiping away sweat, and guzzling iced tea or beer. The sense of community flows like the river, strong and tireless. We won't return the Point to status quo; we'll make it better, thunk-clunk.

As we work, the United States Army steams sedately up the river and stops. That land-based branch of the service does have a few sea- and harbor-going vessels. This one's an LCU—landing craft utility, half the size of the LST that can swallow and transport a tank. She's battleship-grey with a bow like a great, squared-off cliff and a belly that can hold trucks, cranes, and other machines for general maintenance work. We've seen her in the river before, coming in on summer evenings to anchor. The bow ramp would be lowered, and the LCU swarm like an anthill. A gill net would be stretched out for a couple of hours of fishing. She's captained by Tom's brother, a warrant officer. This time, he's come upriver from the port of Morehead not to fish but to see if all's well at the Point after Gloria's attack. Assured that Tom's cottage still stands, he turns the LCU's blunt nose for home.

Tom's captain-brother has also visited the Point less monumentally by way of land, driving in for a week-end with his wife and assorted children. I look at the LCU in the river and hear him in memory's ear. He sits with us in the companionable dark waiting till it's time to boat out with Tom and fetch a net. He stretches and links his hands behind his head, elbows like wings, and says, "This place, you come here and you know what freedom is."

Another block of brick hits the wheelbarrow. "Aren't we having fun!" Bonnie says, meaning it.

Merle pulls a forearm across her dripping forehead. "You'd think we were having a party."

"We are," I say. "An instant-gratification party. Move a load of junk, see more green grass."

"I swear I never want to live any place else," Bonnie says. "Little places are the friendliest."

7

Everything Flows

SOMEWHERE NEAR THE CREEK men's voices crack loud as rifle shots. My crabpots are fished, their contents cooked, cleaned, and stored in the refrigerator for later picking. I put binoculars around my neck and the tote bag, which holds the bird-guide, over my shoulder. Sal and I set off to make midmorning rounds. We could go in any direction, but the bursts of sound draw me through the woods to the sandy beach. At the fringe of the paper company's plantation on the opposite bank of Courts Creek, I see three men dressed in jeans and t-shirts of bright yellow, red, green. Two wear even brighter bandannas of electric purple. They look like a landing party put ashore by Blackbeard himself, and they're wielding piratical weapons, machetes and bush-axes. They chop and glisten with sweat, they laugh and they curse as they swat at deerflies or trip over vine-covered deadwood. Astonishment assaults me. Till now, the only people I've ever seen on the far side of the creek have been boaters and bathers and families with picnic baskets. These men are clearing away saplings and underbrush. For what?

Sal, raring to investigate the ruckus, crosses the creek before I do. As if they were playing at Statues, the men freeze. The unexpected sight of Doberman has issued a silent command. I roll up my jeans and slosh across through shin-deep water. One of the men manages to talk around clenched teeth: "That dog bite?"

At the sound of his voice, Sal gives her customary signs of friendliness, a tail wag and a grin that really is a grin but shows an unfortunately savage expanse of sharp, white Doberteeth. I've got to let these men thaw. "Not yet," I say and point upriver telling Sally, "This way." Instantly, she turns her attention from the pirates and bounds ahead. Seeing that circumstances have tugged us in this direction, we may as well continue upriver. Dog will examine scent-trails while woman scans the woods for birds and scouts the beach for Indian artifacts.

I hear, then see one of John Lawson's Sweet-singing Birds in the woods—a yellow-throated warbler. On my side of the creek they went into seclusion two weeks ago, stopped singing, stopped flashing their colors high in the pines, so that new-laid eggs might be protected by stillness and silence. Closer at hand, I see that Gloria has excavated and removed a foot-deep portion of the oyster-shell midden. The midden lies in a clay bank, its top covered with sand, humus, and pine straw, and the roots of grasses and pines thread through the tumbled heap. The shells are huge, some as long as my size-eight foot. Probably the creek, or another like it, flowed into the river near this point; such junctions were the sites favored for Indian villages and fishing camps. Pottery was manufactured on the spot and often discarded where it was made. With fish and game to be toted home, why lug along clay pots enclosing air? But though I look for shards, I have a better eye for warblers, and all I can see on the sand are rust-colored clots that look deceptively like bits of fired clay but turn out, at a touch, to be soft mud. Onward Sal and I go, to the private ramp where our lost, four-AM visitors had beached their boat.

A demonic screaming starts and rises to unbearable decibels as we approach the ramp. I clap my hands over my ears and just as quickly lower them to take up the binoculars. Green-backed herons are giving me hell. They're nesting, with a rookery hidden back there in some tree guarded by under-brush and barbed-wire vines. I won't find it today. Sal and I turn back toward home. A flock of late-staying red-breasted mergansers sails by heading silently, imperially upriver.

Something's happened to my eyesight or my intuition. At the oyster midden, the clay shards pop miraculously out amid the clots of mud. I pick up two, four, seven of them, grey-black on one side, rusty-red on the other. It's a basic, everyday earthenware. The clay, tempered with grog—the crushed remains of earlier pots—or with sand and grit, was first molded by hand and then licked into final shape by the application of a paddle wrapped with fabric or cord. The red sides still bear the impressions of cloth or cord. The raw pots were probably fired by being inverted on the ground where wood, brush, or corn stalks were stacked around them and set alight. Who made these pots? Who fished here, who opened the shells of these immense oysters and let the contents slide succulent and salty down their throats? How long ago? I would have put money on three or four hundred years—and lost the bet. Dorothy will later help me assemble a package of artifacts found by the midden—red-and-grey potsherds and some yellow-and-brown-glazed fragments that are not of In-dian manufacture but look like accidental accretions of mod-ern trash. The package also contains the Chief's color photos of the inch-long red arrowhead that Kent found at this site. Off it goes to the state's Office of Archaeology. In two weeks word comes back that the glazed fragments aren't modern at all but date back to John Lawson's day, to the 1700s and possi-bly earlier. They're pieces of an earthenware chamber pot, one of such poor grade that I imagine it as used by farm workers rather than the gentlemanly minion of the Lords Proprietors. The potsherds are much older than we'd guessed; they're prehistoric, made by Indians of the hunting-gathering-horticultural Middle Woodland Period that spanned the millennium between 200 BC and AD 800. As for the arrowhead, it's not an arrowhead at all but a projectile point struck from a nodule of jasper and later affixed to a hand-hurled weapon. It's still as sharp as on the day that it was made, and that day was so long ago that when we see its time frame, the prickles rise on the napes of our necks: Archaic Period, 8000 to 4000 BC The archaeologist writes, "Since the point is considerably older than the pottery, it is either an indication of an earlier occupation at the same site or a 'keepsake' item found and maybe used by the later occupants." Whatever its past uses, it is truly a keepsake now. I do not send oyster shells in the package, but the dating for the pottery implies that they, too, may have seen more years than Methuselah.

In the noontime heat that's loud with pirate-yells and the buzz of deerflies, I pluck an old giant of a shell from the midden and stash it with the potsherds in my shoulder-tote. I see what I should have noticed earlier. Those who follow John Lawson's trade have been at work: unweathered wooden stakes, all bearing numbers, have been driven at neat, unobtrusive intervals amid the vines and brush covering the soil a few yards inland from the river. Surveyors for the timber company have cut this plantation into lots. The pirates at the creek are felling small live oaks along with gums and pines, to clear the land. Soon, we'll see a new crop—houses.

Later, the neighbor who has seen the two painter cubs says, "It's the paper companies have kept us isolated all these years. Now they've got a gold mine on their hands."

Still later, a spokesman for the company's real-estate department says, "Values—river lots have become valuable to the point that it's not economical to continue them in tree growing. But we still own several thousand acres on your peninsula that we'll keep in trees."

Change is in the forecast for the Point's weather. On our living room wall beside the modern weather-station, thermometer-barometer-hygrometer, the Chief has hung an old-fashioned weather glass, the sort that Blackbeard or Arthur Barlowe might have tacked up by the ship's helm. It's a large bubble of blown glass suspended from a wrought-iron bracket. Like a long, lazy S, a narrow spout curves upward from the bubble's bottom. The bubble has been half-filled with water tinted my favorite color, the red-orange of an autumn sunset. This simple instrument provides no readings in milli-bars, but it's as accurate a barometer as any for a quick eye-assessment of conditions in the immediate vicinity. When pressure rises, the water is forced down the spout; when it falls, the water moves upward fast or slowly, according to the speed of change. And when the pressure drops precipitously, warning that a frog-drowner or a Gloria may loom, the water spills over and slides down the spout to drip-drip-drip onto a small tray affixed to the iron bracket. If we had such a glass to measure changes in the Point's human pressures, its flame-colored liquid would be rising rapidly, would soon be running over, nor could a small tray hold the flood.

On imagination's lightning express, I journey from Summer-Country back to the other country, archaic Greece, that I try to know by heart. The philosopher Herakleitos speaks from the farther shore of the fifth century BC "Everything flows; nothing remains." His tone is calm and assured; the words allow no dispute.

And I think of rivers as they were anciently sung by the Greeks, by Homer and Pindar, Aeschylus and Euripides— rivers oiled to glistening by sunlight; rivers that launch ships and inseminate the fields making them fat with grass; rivers with waterfall voices that roar the messages of gods; virile rivers that father sons on mortal women; vengeful rivers that flex their rippling muscles and strike out, killing men. Sacred rivers, due infinite respect and all the reverence accorded gods because they couple bounty with capricious might and they flow as evidence of unseen powers unimaginably more durable than flesh and bone. Those Greeks believed that rivers are alive, not just with the myriad creatures that their waters nourish but alive in themselves to the last drop. The Indians of our river would have concurred. I've also heard this belief expressed devoutly at the Point but in shy whispers indicating that such a notion might be thought eccentric, aberrant, absurd by the legions who do not live with River as a fact of daily life.

The spokesman for the timber company's real-estate department says, "People that tend to buy waterfront are usually very sensitive to it." He's probably right. One reason is that natural waters are much in the forefront of the news these days. Public and private bodies cry loudly for preservation, conservation, protection, restoration of the cleanliness that the Indians and Barlowe and Lawson knew. The state adds legislative clout to the demands, though never enough money for all-out enforcement. With tighter strictures on the disposal of wastes, with sterner limits on the catches and the mandating of devices to free sea turtles and too-small crabs from traps, with official emphasis on saving wetland nurseries, on keeping shores clear of erosion-causing bulkheads, the river's vitality has already been enhanced, and its ability to nurture its children. It flows and will flow, ticking to the seasonal rhythms of its own clock. And it will keep on flowing through the people who live here, old-timers and newcomers alike, as blood flows bearing life-breath from the lungs.

It's not the river that's changing, though, so much as the frontier, this latest in the long succession at the Point. Already wilderness has given way. Land cleared for houses means loss of habitat for creatures. The needlerushes have been cut down on the far side of the creek and pond where clapper rail camouflaged themselves and young mud snakes played hide-and-seek, their dark backs striped with orange-yellow that imitates the glint of light on rush-shadowed water. The pair of osprey building at river's edge near the oyster-shell midden have been dislodged, their nest-tree felled.

Wildlife—prime attractions drawing people to the woods

157

and water, but no one can yet say what fate spins slowly on its thread above the river's birds and beasts. It may be that none of us—not animals, not needlerush and pines and live-oaks, not people—have long leaseholds on this land. Only the water's children may gain new kingdoms. We've seen the river's caprice and its appetite—Miss Carrie's vanished fields of corn, the Nay-Sayer's eroding and unrecoverable shore, Gloria's sharp teeth. Since the pirates first began to hack and slash on the far side of the creek, the midden of oyster shells has disappeared into the craw of a nor'easter.

People may be sensitive to waterfront, as the real-estate department's spokesman says, but waterfront ignores humanity. And lately, scientists make educated forecasts that land now water-laved will be water-covered. They cite the greenhouse effect—the accumulation in the atmosphere of pollutants that trap heat around the earth as an afghan traps body-heat on winter nights. Since the ending of the last ice age about fifteen thousand years ago, global sea level has risen steadily with the release of water from receding ice caps. Now, with heat blanketing the planet, there seems to be an acceleration in the rate of rise. The least optimistic experts say that low coastlines around the world will be inundated in thirty to fifty years. Here, it is predicted that the engorged Neuse will flood the Point, the burgeoning real-estate developments, the whole peninsula. We won't be up the creek so much as in it, treading water all the way to Harlowe. But others say that water will rise more patiently or that it may not drown us after all.

Whatever sea level does or does not do, the Point faces another rise, one as certain as the turning of the earth, one that's happening not in tomorrow's crystal ball but right now. The people-level is inching—no, surging—upward. The twenty-four expensive lots on the far side of the creek have begun to lure them. The three-hundred-lot development now underway a little farther upriver will add to the crowd. The river will quickly set the newcomers to its own time, nor

158

would we who are here now wish to deny others the chance to measure their days by sun and moon, migrating birds and the running of the fish. And when the human influx comes, as it shall in its own unstoppable wave, material changes—traffic, municipal services, schools, even a shopping mall of far more elegance than the Harlowe dump—will wash in on the rising water and stay like wrack on the shores of our lives.

The frontier at the Point faces end to its long isolation. We shall become visible, no longer able to lie low and solve problems intimately. Will the newcomers to the river be as cussedly practical and self-reliant as my tiny nation? As blue-blazes independent? As sharp-edged in their goodness? I don't know. I do know at last that I'm not a rhinestone reflecting light but good for little else. Greeks, the Neusiok and the Tuscarora, any traditional people in any place at any time, would recognize my function: to catch and reflect the stories before they're lost. Like Miss Carrie, we do what we can.

It is the Moon of Jumping Mullet, the females heavy with sacs of orange roe as fat as a man's thumb, the males equally round-bellied with white roe, as their milt is called. The water has taken on a post-equinoctial chill. Soon, the first sea-ducks, the black scoter, will raft in; soon, we'll hear the throaty warble of wintering loons. Tonight, the nets are set for whatever the dark river brings. There is an absence among us: Tom's fishing friend Burt, the man for poplar-leaf snakes and moonshine sweetened with hard rock candy, the peanut-eater who's heaped the grass with a hurricane-rubble of peanut shells, the scrounger who conned his trash-man out of the large orange barrels that hold our nets. Burt came as usual to fish with us two weeks ago but excused himself last week account of feeling poorly. Three days ago he died, aged seventy-one-and-a-half. We mourn and honor him by doing what we've always done on Friday nights.

Tom and his LCU-captain brother, clad in oilskins against boat-created spray and a light but winter-bearing wind, bring in the nets one at a time. Other fishing friends, Marines from Tom's department at Cherry Point, pull the catch from the meshes. Scalers in hand, knives newly-whetted by the Chief, the women—Merle, Bonnie and K.D., the captain's wife, and I—stand at the cleaning table, perfect mermaids. On the river anything is possible, even mermaids who wear their scales on windbreakers.

As we dress the fish—blues, spot, roe-bearing mullet, a few grey trout that autumn has summoned back to the river, I glance at industrious hands and listen to the voices of friends lightly telling Burt-stories. Beneath the reminiscences, above and all around them, the river's voice sounds gentle and comforting as it talks to the bulkheads in a soft, persistent whisper. The last net has been boated in, and Tom's captain-brother brings us another dishpan brimming with fish. I remember that here in this yard, on a warmer evening, the captain spoke of the liberty afforded at the Point.

He put the word to it. Here, for this fluid moment, our lives define freedom.

C. 1

2-91   10/96
             3 ᒫ 98